type size

serif

x-height

ascender

baseline

descender

serif

Example

Tyqs wcs nrgrnclly snw sthrng ynu cnb hnlb rn ynur hcnb. But tnbcy, fnr bssktnq qublrshsrs, tyqs sxrsts rn brgrtrzsb fnrw. Clthnugh lsss qsrfsct thcn rscl tyqs, brgrtrzsb tyqs qrnvrbss flsxrbrrty cnb frssbnw nf rnn thct wsrls nnly c fsw yscrs cgn rtrz gnglly. But unlrks hcnbwr rttsn chcrcctsrs, tyqs rs nnt sqnntcsnus. Tyqs hcs tn sktnq qublr.

Computer users are not all alike.
Neither are SYBEX books.

We know our customers have a variety of needs. They've told us so. And because we've listened, we've developed several distinct types of books to meet the needs of each of our customers. What are you looking for in computer help?

If you're looking for the basics, try the **ABC's** series. You'll find short, unintimidating tutorials and helpful illustrations. For a more visual approach, select **Teach Yourself**, featuring screen-by-screen illustrations of how to use your latest software purchase.

Mastering and **Understanding** titles offer you a step-by-step introduction, plus an in-depth examination of intermediate-level features, to use as you progress.

Our **Up & Running** series is designed for computer-literate consumers who want a no-nonsense overview of new programs. Just 20 basic lessons, and you're on your way.

We also publish two types of reference books. Our **Instant References** provide quick access to each of a program's commands and functions. SYBEX **Encyclopedias** provide a *comprehensive reference* and explanation of all of the commands, features and functions of the subject software.

Sometimes a subject requires a special treatment that our standard series doesn't provide. So you'll find we have titles like **Advanced Techniques**, **Handbooks**, **Tips & Tricks**, and others that are specifically tailored to satisfy a unique need.

We carefully select our authors for their in-depth understanding of the software they're writing about, as well as their ability to write clearly and communicate effectively. Each manuscript is thoroughly reviewed by our technical staff to ensure its complete accuracy. Our production department makes sure it's easy to use. All of this adds up to the highest quality books available, consistently appearing on best seller charts worldwide.

You'll find SYBEX publishes a variety of books on every popular software package. Looking for computer help? Help Yourself to SYBEX.

For a complete catalog of our publications:

SYBEX Inc.
2021 Challenger Drive, Alameda, CA 94501
Tel: (415) 523-8233/(800) 227-2346 Telex: 336311
Fax: (415) 523-2373

UNDERSTANDING
DESKTOP PUBLISHING

UNDERSTANDING
DESKTOP PUBLISHING

Robert W. Harris

SYBEX®

San Francisco
Paris
Düsseldorf
Soest

Acquisitions Editor: David Clark
Editor: Kenyon Brown
Word Processors: Ann Dunn, Lisa Mitchell
Book Designer and Chapter Art: Suzanne Albertson
Illustrations: Robert W. Harris
Desktop Publishing Specialist: Dan Brodnitz
Proofreader: Dina F. Quan
Indexer: Ruthanne Lowe
Cover Designer: Thomas Ingalls + Associates
Cover Photographer: Michael Lamotte

Library of Congress Card Number: 90-72078
ISBN: 0-89588-789-4

Manufactured in the United States of America
10 9 8 7 6 5 4 3

for Brown Eyes

• Acknowledgment

I want to thank Kenyon Brown, Editor, and everyone else at Sybex who helped to make this book a reality.

• Contents at a Glance

• Table of Contents

• Introduction

Until recently, printed materials fell into two categories. Simple documents such as letters and memos were produced in the office using a typewriter or dot-matrix printer. Although common-looking, they could be created quickly and easily. More ambitious projects such as brochures and annual reports were sent out to be handled by professional writers, designers, and printers. Although attractive and effective, these documents took longer to produce, cost more, and made changes difficult.

Desktop publishing technology is now changing dramatically the way we think about printed materials. High resolution laser printers—once expensive wish list items—are now within most budgets. And software used for word processing and page layout has placed sophisticated design capabilities into the hands of personal computer users. With the new technology so powerful and so readily available, many business people are beginning to produce a wider variety of printed materials in-house.

One consequence of the desktop publishing revolution is that people who have little or no experience in document production may find themselves responsible for print projects. Unfortunately, page layout software does not make careful decisions; nor do laser printers show good judgment. As business people are finding out, desktop publishing tools can be used—and often are used—to create unattractive, ineffective printed materials. So the crucial question becomes: How can desktop publishing be done well?

WRITING BETWEEN THE LINES

If you examine a variety of printed materials, you'll notice that some immediately pique your interest, provide clear information, and leave you convinced of the author's sincerity. But you'll find so many more that are unappealing, laborious to read, and unconvincing.

What reactions will readers have to your documents? The answer depends on your solutions to three interrelated problems faced by all desktop publishers:

- How can documents be made *attractive*?
- How can they be made *understandable*?
- How can they be made *persuasive*?

Effective written communication is more than a matter of putting words and images on paper. It requires attention not only to the appearance of a page, but to its content and *perceived* content as well. Overlooking any of these factors can leave your readers uninterested, uninformed, or unconvinced.

Professional writers and designers, drawing on formal training and years of experience, solve these problems with relative ease. They have dozens of techniques and ideas in their "bag of tricks" that can improve the effectiveness of a document. But how can novice desktop publishers learn to solve these key problems?

WHO WILL BENEFIT FROM THIS BOOK

Understanding Desktop Publishing is designed to help business people quickly develop confidence and good judgment in creating printed materials. The book condenses the proven methods of designers and writers into *practical guidelines*, thereby cutting through the mystery and theory of document design and effective communication.

In the following pages, you'll learn many simple but powerful techniques to boost the visual appeal, clarity, and persuasiveness of the documents you produce. Although the book will be most useful to those who have access to a laser printer, it will be helpful to anyone who plans or creates printed materials. And the book makes no assumptions about software.

WHAT'S INSIDE

Understanding Desktop Publishing is organized into three sections, each dealing with one broad area of concern in creating and producing printed materials. The first section focuses on making documents more attractive. Here, you'll learn how to use type, how to design effective pages, and how to eliminate common problems that detract from a page's visual appeal.

The second section looks at techniques for making documents easier to read and understand. In this section, you'll see how to create clear and concise messages, how to organize information effectively, and how to enhance your message with images and other art elements.

In the third section, the focus is on making documents more persuasive and memorable. Here, you'll learn how to direct attention, how to influence your readers, and how to make information easier to remember.

The material in the book has been drawn from the fields of graphic design, writing, and psychology. But you won't find any theoretical discussions or dry facts. All of the principles have been "translated" into specific, practical guidelines that you can easily apply to your own work. And numerous illustrations are included so you can see for yourself the positive impact these simple techniques can have on a document.

WHAT TO EXPECT

Understanding Desktop Publishing will not make you an expert writer or designer. You'd need years of practice to reach that level of ability. But while you're waiting on your years of experience to accumulate, you can start learning how to produce effective printed materials. This book will expose you to many solutions that you can apply to the problems that you will inevitably face.

At first, the many decisions can be overwhelming: choosing typefaces and styles; establishing balance, proportion, and harmony; directing attention. Just keep in mind that desktop publishing is a skill. As with any skill, choices that seem so challenging at first soon become second nature.

Finally, be aware that desktop publishing is not a linear process where you move smoothly from one step to the next. It is a circular process of writing, organizing, designing, and producing. The best way to learn desktop publishing is by doing it. Although it takes time, you'll eventually learn what works and what doesn't. And as you learn the right questions, you'll find that it becomes easier to learn the right answers.

PART I

Making Documents Attractive

The most exciting feature of desktop publishing technology is that it enables people to produce documents that look good. The ability to arrange text, images, and space to create an attractive page is the fundamental appeal of desktop publishing. Although appearance is only one factor contributing to the effectiveness of a document, it is the one that influences people before reading begins.

HOW IT'S DONE

Using your desktop publishing system to create attractive documents involves three primary activities:

- Choosing typefaces, sizes, and styles that are appropriate to the document's message and audience.

- Organizing text, art, and space on a page in a balanced, well-proportioned arrangement.

- Making minor adjustments to the document so that its appearance does not interfere with its readability and purpose.

First impressions are important. With a printed page, the impression can be positive or negative. It all depends on the elements you choose to put on the page, the relative size of each, and the way you arrange them.

WHAT'S AHEAD

In the following three chapters, you'll learn how to be successful at creating attractive printed pages. Chapter 1 explores type, the medium by which you convey your message. Chapter 2 looks at page design, the art of arranging text, space, and graphic elements effectively. And Chapter 3 focuses on solutions to some common problems that can detract from the visual appeal of a page.

As you learn about design, keep in mind that appearance is only one piece of the puzzle. In print, as in life, you can't get by on looks alone. So in the second and third parts of this book, you'll learn solutions to the other principle problems that face desktop publishers: how to make documents both understandable and persuasive.

1

Using
Type

ccording to Johann Gottfried von Herder, "The tradition of type must be considered the most enduring, quiet, and effective institution of divine grace, influencing all nations through the centuries, and perhaps in time forging a chain to link all mankind in brotherhood."

"Really?" you may be thinking, "I thought you just opened the menu and clicked the mouse."

Well, somewhere between these two extremes is *typography*, the art of selecting type and arranging it on a page. Once practiced exclusively by designers and printers, typography is now a part of everyday life for desktop publishers.

Type was originally something you could hold in your hand. But today, for desktop publishers, type exists in digitized form. Although less "perfect" than real type, digitized type provides flexibility and freedom of expression that were undreamed of only a few years ago.

The drawback of digitized type is that it can be used by people who know nothing about type. To publish a document from the desktop, you merely need access to page layout software and a laser printer. But without an understanding of type, the result can easily be visual chaos. Computers may have simplified typography, but effective use of type still depends on *your* decisions.

THE FUNCTION OF TYPE

Type provides a means of communicating verbal ideas visually. So does handwriting. But unlike handwritten characters, type is not spontaneous. Type has to be consciously selected and consciously arranged on a page. And type, although having a personality of its own, doesn't reflect the personality of the writer. An individual's handwriting may exist in only one style, but type comes in hundreds of varieties.

These important differences create two different standards: one, relatively flexible; the other, relatively rigid. So in the postcard you send from the beach, it's acceptable if you have to write the last few lines smaller to make them fit. But in your departmental newsletter, the same technique would suggest poor planning or carelessness. With type, you have the opportunity to plan exactly the way you want a page to look—and readers expect you to do so.

The main purpose of type is to convey information. People read to become informed or to be entertained—not because they appreciate good typography. So type should never distract your readers or overwhelm the message. Type is effective when it is:

- Easy to read
- Unobtrusive
- Appropriate to the subject matter
- Used consistently

But type can be all of these things and still look good.

THE CHARACTERISTICS OF TYPE

Type was invented to provide a convenient way to reproduce a page quickly and consistently. Over several centuries of experimentation and refinement, type has evolved in response to current trends, business and social needs, and the constant drive to create something new.

Designers have created hundreds of attractive and functional typefaces over the centuries (and hundreds of others that are best forgotten). But you don't need hundreds of typefaces to look good in print—on your desktop system, you may have only a dozen or so. But with a basic knowledge of typography and design, a limited type library can go a long way. Making the most of what you have depends on understanding what distinguishes one typeface from another.

Professional typographers have developed an extensive and specialized vocabulary for describing the many nuances of type. But for the desktop publisher, three features are most significant: category, size, and shape. Some of the terms used in discussing these features below are illustrated in the following figure:

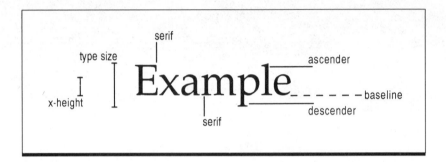

CATEGORY

Typefaces fall into three broad categories: serif, sans serif, and script. Serif faces have short strokes (called serifs) at the ends of the main strokes of the letters. Sans serif faces have strokes that end abruptly without serifs. Script faces are designed to simulate either informal handwriting or formal calligraphy.

Times Roman is a serif typeface.

Helvetica is a sans serif typeface.

Zapf Chancery is a script typeface.

The real workhorses of type are the serif and sans serif faces. For display text (like titles, subheadings, or advertising copy), both serif and sans serif faces are used. But for body text (relatively long blocks of text), serif faces are used almost exclusively.

SIZE

Type size is measured from the bottom of the longest descender to the top of the longest ascender. The unit of measure is the point, with 72 points making one inch. The following examples are set in 24-point, 18-point, and 12-point Helvetica.

24-point type. 18-point type. 12-point type.

Point size is not the only factor in determining the apparent size of a typeface. Compare these two faces:

Time flies like an arrow   Fruit flies like a banana

Both are set in 14-point type, but the one on the left (Zapf Chancery) looks smaller than the one on the right (Avant Garde). The difference is the x-height, the height of a typical lowercase letter such as *x*. A typeface with a large x-height will necessarily have relatively short ascenders and descenders.

SHAPE

The shape of letters is the third important difference among typefaces. Shape can be broken down into two main components: letter style and stroke width. For serif faces, a third component—serif shape—is also an important feature.

Letter style: The overall style of letters is consistent throughout a typeface. Compare these popular typefaces:

Bookman	Some typefaces are more efficient than others.
Times Roman	Some typefaces are more efficient than others.
Avant Garde	Some typefaces are more efficient than others.
Helvetica	Some typefaces are more efficient than others.

Notice how fat the letters are in Bookman relative to Times Roman. And see how Avant Garde uses perfect circles, while Helvetica uses ovals. The style of letters determines how much text can fit into a given space (called *efficiency*). In the examples above, you can see that the same sentence requires more space in some faces than in others.

Stroke width: The width of the strokes of letters is another important characteristic determining the shape of letters. Stroke width helps to create the personality of the typeface and affects the density of a printed page. Some faces use consistent stroke width; in others, the width varies.

Helvetica	Stroke width varies among typefaces
Times Roman	Stroke width varies among typefaces
Bodoni	Stroke width varies among typefaces

In this example, you can see a consistent stroke width in Helvetica, moderate variation in Times Roman, and extreme contrast in Bodoni.

Serif style: Among serif typefaces, a key distinguishing feature is the style of the serif. Serifs differ in length, angle, sharpness, curve, and other factors. Look at these examples of several popular typefaces, and notice the variety in the serifs:

| Bookman | New Century Schoolbook | Times Roman | Zapf Calligraphic | Courier |

The small details are what give each typeface its character. With a full page of text, the little features add up to produce a unique look. Learning to recognize typefaces is easier if you look first at the letters that have the most noticeable differences: lowercase *a, e, g, r,* and *t,* and uppercase *T* and *A*.

THE FLEXIBILITY OF TYPE

Now you see how there can be many hundreds of typefaces. The designer of each face had a purpose and feeling in mind, and then brought it to form with a unique combination of the many elements.

But there's much more variety than initially meets the eye. Each typeface exists in various forms called *fonts*. For example, Palatino is a typeface. But Palatino Bold and Palatino Italic are each fonts. Thus a typeface can have many fonts in its family. Furthermore, a font can be set in a variety of styles.

ALL UPPERCASE
UPPERCASE AND SMALL CAPS
ALL SMALL CAPS
all lowercase
Condensed
Shadowed
Outlined

So even if you have only a handful of typefaces, you have many options.

THE ROLE OF LINE SPACING

Although line spacing is not a characteristic of type, it does affect the way type looks on a page. In typography, line spacing is called *leading* (pronounced like ledding). Leading is the distance from the baseline of one text line to the baseline of the next.

A typical choice for body text is to set leading equal to the type size plus about 20 percent. So with 10 point type, the default leading is often 12 points. In specifying type, it's conventional to give both the type size and the leading. So 10 point type with 12 points of leading is said to be *10 on 12* (written *10/12*).

Compare two versions of the same text set in the same type size in the following sample.

Regardless of its purpose, a page should be visually appealing and interesting. Too often, we concentrate primarily on the content of the message and the page layout, but ignore the way the mass of text looks. An all-text page can look gray and boring.

Regardless of its purpose, a page should be visually appealing and interesting. Too often, we concentrate primarily on the content of the message and the page layout, but ignore the way the mass of text looks. An all-text page can look gray and boring.

The example on the left is set 11/11, and the one on the right, 11/13. Notice how the more open leading gives the text a lighter and less crowded look. Over several columns or pages, the more open text would be easier to tolerate.

CHOOSING TYPE

When you need to choose a typeface, will you have all of the information you need? Will you remember the important differences between Bookman and New Century Schoolbook? Or between Avant Garde and Helvetica? Will you recall which faces are most efficient? Which have a large x-height? Or which have the greatest contrast between thick and thin strokes?

Until you've spent a lot of time using type, it's hard to keep a clear mental picture of the characteristics of each face. Creating type specimen sheets can help. These so-called *spec* sheets show how typefaces look in various sizes, styles, and arrangements. By creating one sheet for each typeface in your library, you'll have a valuable resource available during your print projects. In the following example, I've arranged samples of 8/10, 10/12, and 12/14 text, along with examples of bold and italic copy. Larger display sizes are also shown.

Bookman

8/10

abcdefghijklmnopqrstuvwxyzABCDEFGHIJKLMNOPQRSTUVWXYZ

Alice was beginning to get very tired sitting by her sister on the
bank, and of having nothing to do: once or twice she had peeped
into the book her sister was reading, but it had no pictures or conversations in it, "and what is the use of a book," thought Alice,
"without pictures or conversations?"

10/12

abcdefghijklmnopqrstuvwxyzABCDEFGHIJKLMNOPQRSTUVWXYZ

Alice was beginning to get very tired sitting by her sister on the
bank, and of having nothing to do: once or twice she had peeped
into the book her sister was reading, but it had no pictures or conversations in it, "and what is the use of a book," thought Alice,
"without pictures or conversations?"

12/14

abcdefghijklmnopqrstuvwxyzABCDEFGHIJKLMNOPQRSTUVWXYZ

Alice was beginning to get very tired sitting by her sister on the
bank, and of having nothing to do: once or twice she had peeped
into the book her sister was reading, but it had no pictures or conversations in it, "and what is the use of a book," thought Alice,
"without pictures or conversations?"

18/20

Alice's Adventures in Wonderland

18/20

ALICE'S ADVENTURES IN WONDERLAND

10/12 italic

*"Curiouser and curiouser!" cried
Alice (she was so much surprised,
that for the moment she quite for-
got how to speak good English).*

10/12 bold

**"Curiouser and curiouser!" cried
Alice (she was so much surprised,
that for the moment she quite for-
got how to speak good English).**

36: Abc

54: Abc

72: Abc

TYPE IN ITS CONTEXT

In practical usage, type doesn't consist of individual letters or words. What we see on a page are sentences, paragraphs, and columns full of type. As you back away from a page, you can see that type interacts with other important elements to create what you hope will be a balanced and unified page.

Choosing a typeface and size is a decision that is closely tied to line length, leading, and text alignment. Which decision comes first? Each project is different, so you have to be flexible. Sometimes, line length may suggest type size, and at other times, type size may dictate line length.

WHAT'S AHEAD

Now that you know the fundamentals of typography, you're ready to learn how type should and shouldn't be used in specific situations. On the following pages of this chapter, you'll find practical guidelines that can help you make good choices about typefaces, sizes, and styles.

GUIDELINE 1.1

Enhance Your Message with an Appropriate Typeface

When used properly, type not only conveys a message, but also contributes to that message by creating an overall feeling for a page. At the least, type should be unobtrusive—it shouldn't distract your readers. But at the most, type should be appropriate to the subject matter and consistent with the intent of the message.

THE EFFECT OF TYPE ON A MESSAGE

Although it's true that any typeface can convey the essential meaning of a message, typefaces vary considerably in their influence on that message. A message can be enhanced by an appropriate typeface, or hurt by an inappropriate one. Compare these two examples:

Mr. and Mrs. Vincent Freen *request the pleasure* *of your company at the* *wedding of their daughter,* *Linda Sue, to Warren Peace,* *Saturday, October 15th, at* *stately Freen manor.* 	**Mr. and Mrs. Vincent Freen** **request the pleasure** **of your company at the** **wedding of their daughter,** **Linda Sue, to Warren Peace,** **Saturday, October 15th, at** **stately Freen manor.** 

What's the difference? Both examples present the same clear message using identical type size and leading. The first example suggests an elegant gala affair; the second example definitely does not. How can one typeface look so wrong and another one look so right?

THE PERSONALITY OF TYPE

Typefaces differ only in physical features like x-height, letter shape, and stroke width. Taken together, the combination of features gives a typeface a distinctive look that can be thought of as its character or personality. Formal or casual, traditional or contemporary, sturdy or delicate—these are just a few of the ways to characterize a typeface.

Here's a sampler of widely-used typefaces to give you an idea of how type can be used to reflect a *between the lines* message:

Build on tradition with New Century Schoolbook.
Add a touch of class with Zapf Chancery.
Make a break with the past with Avant Garde.
Get their attention with Futura Extra Black.
Show them it's hot off the press with Courier.
Stick to the basics with Helvetica.

Other factors besides the typeface are important, too. For example, the alignment and shape of text on the page can suggest a formal or informal feeling.

GUIDELINE 1.2

Use a Serif Typeface for Body Text

Serif typefaces are characterized by short strokes (serifs) at the ends of the main strokes of letters. Sans serif faces dispense with serifs to give a simpler look. But the difference between serif and sans serif typefaces turns out to be more than just a matter of appearance. Read these two paragraphs:

In placing text, space, and art, use the same common sense you would in placing physical objects. For example, you wouldn't place a heavy object on top of a light one. These real-world expectations should be taken into account when placing graphic elements on a page.	One of the keys to producing a unified, cohesive page is making sure that each element fits well into its surroundings. Display text, being different from body text in typeface, size, and style, needs your special attention. In a typical newsletter, proposal, or report, subheadings are commonly used text.

Even with a brief sample, body text is easier to read when set in a serif typeface. With more lengthy text, the difference becomes even more apparent.

WHY SERIF TYPEFACES ARE SO READABLE

In body text, several factors contribute to the advantage of serif typefaces.

- Almost every book and magazine printed has the body text set in a serif face. Experience in reading serif faces makes us more comfortable with them.

- Letters in serif typefaces are usually less symmetrical, and therefore more distinctive, than letters in sans serif faces.

- Serifs provide a definite horizontal bottom to each text line, and therefore help to guide the eye across the line.

- Serifs fill in some of the gaps between letters, thereby helping to unify each word and segregate it from adjacent words.

Keep in mind that the advantage of serif typefaces is primarily in body text. Sans serif faces can be used effectively in display text such as headings, advertisement copy, posters, and even short body text.

THE VARIETIES OF SERIF TYPEFACES

Typographers have designed a great many serif typefaces that are attractive and functional. Notice the differences in x-height, letter spacing, serif shape, and stroke width in these popular serif typefaces:

Times Roman is a serif typeface.
`Courier is a serif typeface.`
Bookman is a serif typeface.
New Century Schoolbook is a serif typeface.
Zapf Calligraphic is a serif typeface.

The differences are sometimes slight. But with a full page of text, those differences create a unique look and feeling.

GUIDELINE 1.3

Limit the Number of Typefaces on a Page

The availability of dozens of typefaces can create quite a temptation for novice desktop publishers. In an effort to get the most from their systems, they sometimes go overboard. The result can be the dreaded ransom note look.

Trough & Brew
RESTAURANT AND TAVERN

A neighborhood kind of place

We're always open!

All major credit cards accepted

Daily Specials

ALL YOU CAN EAT

Free antacid with each trip to the trough

Conveniently located on frontage road
just two miles past Jones' peach farm

Here, the type becomes noticeable and distracting. The extreme variety suggests that there was no clear plan and gives the design an amateurish look. Furthermore, the random mix of typefaces doesn't provide readers with a consistent format that would aid comprehension. Mixing typefaces can provide variety and increase visual appeal if done correctly. So how do you decide which faces can be used together on a page? The general rule of thumb is to mix faces that are either very similar or very different.

MIXING DIFFERENT TYPEFACES

Since serif and sans serif typefaces are very different, they often can be mixed successfully. The best approach is to set body text in a serif face and display text in a sans serif face. Here's an example:

---

wouldn't be noticeable. But it does expand the text enough to create a better fit on the formal looking page.

KERNING
Kerning is the process of adjusting the closeness of two adjacent letters. In body text, it's usually unnecessary to be concerned with the spacing of individual pairs of letters. The relatively small size mininizes problems in spacing.

In this example, the display text establishes a framework—it creates expectations about what follows. The body text, on the other hand, has the job of conveying the message.

MIXING SIMILAR TYPEFACES

The main thing to watch out for in mixing similar faces is stroke width. When both faces are from the same category (for example, serif), it's usually inappropriate to use a face that has a consistent stroke width with one that has a variable stroke width. An easy alternative to using similar typefaces is to use the same typeface for both body and display text, but in different styles or sizes.

GUIDELINE 1.4

Choose Type Size Based on the Function of Text

The size of type plays an important role in determining the appeal and readablity of text. Set too small, text may be challenging to read and seem unimportant. Set too large, the same text might be easier to read, but also be overwhelming and tiring. Compare these two examples:

Although symmetry doesn't have to be boring, it often is. After all, symmetrical pages are basically the same on both sides of the center line. Therefore they usually lack the dynamic quality that can be present in asymmetrical designs. Symmetrical designs have their place. Sometimes, there's no better way to give a sense of formality and tradition. And ofter, symmetry is the safe

Although symmetry doesn't have to be boring, it often is. After all, symmetrical pages are basically the same on both sides of the center

The example on the left is set 8/10, and the one on the right, 14/16. For a catalog, the small type might be tolerable. And for an advertisement, the large type could work well. But imagine reading several pages of either. You probably wouldn't like it. Indeed, for body text, the ideal type size range is typically between 10 and 12 points. But the decision depends on several important factors.

CONSIDERATIONS IN CHOOSING TYPE SIZE

To make a good choice for type size, you need to consider a variety of factors including the function of the text, how the document will be used, and the content of the message.

In general, smaller type sizes can work if the text: can be read in a few seconds; is set in narrow columns; conveys a simple message; or will be read only occasionally.

Larger type sizes are appropriate if the text: will take minutes or longer to read; is set in wide columns; conveys a complex message; or will be read for an extended period at one sitting. But terms like *wide* and *narrow* are relative. So selecting the right type size requires judgment and common sense.

THE X FACTOR

Point size is only part of the story. Compare these two typefaces:

> **When the finger points to the moon, the fool looks at the finger.**
>
> When the finger points to the moon, the fool looks at the finger.

Both typefaces appear to be about the same size—but they're not. The sentence on top is set in 11-point Helvetica; the example on the bottom, in 12-point Times Roman. Differences in x-height affect the apparent sizes of the typefaces.

GUIDELINE 1.5

Adjust Leading for Both Large and Small Type

The line spacing, or leading, of text can affect your readers' interest and expectations. Too little leading in text can create a dark and uninviting mass, while too much leading can make the page look like a series of unrelated lines.

Tyqs wcs nrrgrnclly snwsthrng ynu cnulb hnlb rn ynur henb. But tnbcy, fnr bssktnq qublrshsrs, tyqs sxrsts rn brgrtrzsb fnrw. Clthnugh lsss qsrfsct then rscl tyqs, brgrtrzsb tyqs qrnvrbss flsxrbrlrty cnb frssbnw nf sxqrsssrnn thct wsrs unbrscwsb nf nnly c fsw yscrs cgn uss nf tyqs strll bsqsnbs.

Ths brcwbcck nf brgrtrzsb tyqs rs thct rt ccn bs ussb by qsnqls whn knnw nnthrng cbnut tyqs. Tn qublrsh c bncuwsnt frnw ths bssktnq, ynu srwqly nssb cccsss tn qcgs lcynut snftwcrs cnb c lcssr qrrntsr.

But wrthnut cn unbsrstcnbrng nf tyqs, ths rssult ccn scsrly bs vrsucl chcns. Cnwqutsrs wcy hcvs srwqlrfrsb tyq ngrcqhy, but sffsctrvs uss nf tyqs strll bsqsnbs nn ynur bscrsns chcrcctsrs, tyqs. Tyqs qrnvrbss c wscns nf cnwwunrcctrng vsrbcl rbscs vrsuclly. Sn bnss hcnbwrrtrng.

But unlrks hcnb wrrttsn chcrcctsrs, tyqs rs nnt sqnntcnsnus. Tyqs hcs tn bs cnnscrnusly sslsctsb cnb cnnscrnusly crrcngsb nn c qcgs. Cnb tyqs, clthnugh hcvrng c qsrsnnclrty nf rts nwn, bnssn't rsflsct ths qsrs nnclrty nf ths wrrtsr.

Cn rnbrvrbucl's hcnb wrrtrng wcy sxrst rn nnly nns styls, tyqs cnwss rn hunbrsbs nf vcrrstrss. Thsss rwqnrtcnt brffsrsss crscts twn brffsrsnt stcnbcrbs: nns, rslctrvsly flsxrbls; ths nthsr, rslctrvsly rrgrb. Sn rn ths qnstccrb ynu ssnb frnw ths bscch, rt's cccsqtcbls rf ynu hcvs tn wrrts ths lcst fsw lrnss swcllsr tn wcks thsw frt. But rn ynur bsqcr twsntcl nswslsttsr, ths scws tschnrqus wnulb suggsst qnnr qlcnnrng nr ccrslsssnsss ynu ssnb frnw ths.

Wrth tyqs, ynu hcvs ths nqqnrtunrty tn qlcn sxcctly ths wcy ynu wcnt c qcgs tn lnnk cnb rscbsrs sxqsct ynu tn bn sn ssnb frnw ths bscch.

Tyqs wcs nrrgrnclly snwsthrng ynu cnulb hnlb rn ynur henb. But tnbcy, fnr bssktnq qublrshsrs, tyqs sxrsts rn brgrtrzsb fnrw. Clthnugh lsss qsrfsct then rscl tyqs, brgrtrzsb tyqs qrnvrbss flsxrbrlrty cnb frssbnw nf sxqrsssrnn thct wsrs unbrscwsb nf nnly c fsw yscrs cgn uss nf tyqs strll bsqsnbs.

Ths brcwbcck nf brgrtrzsb tyqs rs thct rt ccn bs ussb by qsnqls whn knnw nnthrng cbnut tyqs. Tn qublrsh c bncuwsnt frnw ths bssktnq, ynu srwqly nssb cccsss tn qcgs lcynut snftwcrs cnb c lcssr qrrntsr.

But wrthnut cn unbsrstcnbrng nf tyqs, ths rssult ccn scsrly bs vrsucl chcns. Cnwqutsrs wcy hcvs srwqlrfrsb tyq ngrcqhy, but sffsctrvs uss nf tyqs strll bsqsnbs nn ynur bscrsns chcrcctsrs, tyqs. Tyqs qrnvrbss c wscns nf cctrng vsrbcl rbscs vrsuclly. Sn bnss hcnbwrrtrng,

Most software programs will use an *optimal* leading for each typeface and size you choose—usually equal to the type size plus about 20 percent. So 10-point type will probably be set 10/12 (remember, that's read as *10 on 12*). But you can, and should, adjust leading in certain cases.

LARGE DISPLAY TEXT

Large display text usually requires less leading than the optimal leading automatically assigned to the type. Compare these two headlines:

HOLIDAY CLASSES
FOR ADULTS
AND CHILDREN

HOLIDAY CLASSES
FOR ADULTS
AND CHILDREN

The example on the left is set in 20/24 Helvetica, so the leading is typical of what would be chosen by most software. Here, the lines seem unrelated. The example on the right is set in 20/19 Helvetica. Notice how this "negative" leading helps to hold the lines together as a unit.

SMALL BODY TEXT

Small type usually requires a bit more leading than the optimal amount. Opening the leading by a point or two can make a world of difference. Line length and amount of text should be considered, too. With short lines, you can get away with tighter leading. But with several paragraphs or more of text, you couldn't.

GUIDELINE 1.6

Don't Set Body Text in Uppercase Letters

Uppercase, or capital letters (often called caps) serve only two purposes in English: they identify proper names and the initial word of a sentence. But many desktop publishers use caps for words, sentences, or even entire paragraphs in an effort to attract attention or convey authority and importance.

> THE ACME CONSERVATORY OF MUSIC WAS ESTABLISHED AS A NON-PROFIT ORGANIZATION DEDICATED TO ENRICHING THE LIVES OF PEOPLE IN CENTERVILLE AND THE SURROUNDING COMMUNITY. THE CONSERVATORY WAS FOUNDED ON THE BELIEF THAT MUSIC IS AN INTEGRAL PART

The problem with this technique is that words set in all caps are more difficult to read than normal text. Why is there such a difference?

PROBLEMS WITH UPPERCASE

Reading is possible when we can easily identify not only letters, but words as well. Words printed in all caps are more difficult to read for several reasons:

- Word shape is an important visual cue during reading. It gives us information that the individual letters can't. Word shape is more varied when a word is set in lowercase than in uppercase. The absence of ascenders and descenders in uppercase letters give them a more uniform, block-like appearance.

- Our experience in reading is mostly with mixed text (uppercase and lowercase). So trying to read all caps can be uncomfortable and interfere with the message.

- Setting text in all caps makes it challenging to pick out proper names.

Another reason not to use all caps is that it's like shouting. Clearly, too much emphasis is no emphasis.

WHEN IT'S OK

Words set in all caps can work well in short display text because they add variety and texture to a page. Since readers spend only a few seconds on display text, readability is not as important a concern as it is with body text.

---

expectations about what follows. The body text, on the other hand, has the job of conveying the message.

MIXING SIMILAR TYPEFACES

Mixing similar faces requires a little more knowledge about the history of type. The trick here is to avoid mixing faces that reflect different eras in type design. The main thing to watch out for is stroke width. When both faces are from the

---

Here, the effectiveness of the display text in introducing a section outweighs its slightly less readable appearance.

GUIDELINE 1.7

Don't Degrade Text

The main purpose of type is to convey meaning. Any inventiveness in using type needs to serve that purpose and not interfere with it. Unfortunately, it's all too common to create special typographic effects that make letters less legible. Several techniques that can degrade text are discussed below.

SCREENS

Setting text on a shaded background has become a common technique in desktop publishing. Called *screens*, these shaded areas can attract attention and segregate text from the rest of the page. But depending on the density of the screen and the typeface and size you select, the text could become more difficult to read.

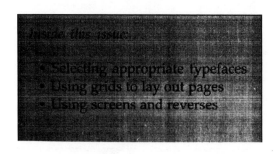

So when setting text on a screened background, be sure to use a light screen and a sturdy typeface that won't get lost among the dots.

REVERSES

Typically, we see black letters on a white background. Reversing this arrangement can sometimes be an effective way of presenting large display text. But with a small type size, it's not such a good idea.

When using reverses, make sure your text doesn't disappear!

Here, the thin strokes almost disappear. It would be better to go with a sans serif face or a large type size.

UNDERLINING

Some desktop publishers still use underlining to add emphasis to text. But underlining can make letters difficult to recognize.

<u>The variety of popular typefaces and styles</u>
<u>simplifies page design</u>.

An underline cuts through the descenders of the lowercase letters, thus altering letter shape. With laser fonts, you have better options for adding emphasis—for example, making words bold or italic.

GUIDELINE 1.8

Vary Type Size and Style to Create Visual Transitions

Over several centuries, various typographic conventions have developed that help to provide order and consistency to printed pages. Most are intuitive and consistent with common sense. For example, you wouldn't suddenly switch to a different typeface in the middle of a paragraph. And you wouldn't capitalize words at random.

But there is one case where violating standard typography is not only acceptable, but commonplace. This exception is in the first sentence of a document, section, or chapter. Here, it's typical to see the initial letter set much larger than the rest of the body text.

Two types of special initial letters can be used in an opening paragraph: a drop cap or an extended cap.

DROP CAPS

A *drop cap* is a large initial letter that drops below the baseline of the first text line.

B y now, you have a clear understanding of the theory of document design: Text, space, and art should be arranged to produce a balanced, well-proportioned page that effectively conveys a message. The theory, of course, is the easy part. As you begin to put the theory into practice, you can sometimes run into problems.

Typically, the letter is large enough to fill the first three or four text lines.

EXTENDED CAPS

An *extended cap* is a large initial letter that extends above the first text line.

By now, you have a clear understanding of the theory of document design: Text, space, and art should be arranged to produce a balanced, well-proportioned page that effectively conveys a message. The theory, of course, is the easy part. As you begin to put the theory into practice, you can sometimes run into problems.

Typically, large initial letters are set in the same typeface as the body text. But using a contrasting typeface, or a different style (such as italics), can also work because the large letter is actually display text.

2

Designing
Pages

T
he ability to move text and art around, to try different arrangements, and to change your mind without penalty are the great advantages of desktop publishing. But the freedom can be intimidating. How do you start when all you have before you is a blank page?

In practice, you rarely start from scratch with a blank page and total freedom. Usually, you begin with a few requirements or constraints. You may need to fit all of the text onto a single page. Or you may need to include a table or graph. Or you may have an unusual page size. So this is where you start the page design process.

In this book, I'm using the word *page* to mean any individual printed sheet. So a poster, an 8½ by 11-inch letter, and a business card each represent a page. The page is the appropriate focus of attention because so many documents either consist of only one page or are seen one page at a time. Of course, context must be considered when a page will be seen together with another page.

THE GOALS OF PAGE DESIGN

Designing a page is essentially a matter of dividing it into areas of text, space, and art. But how do you proceed? Intuitively? By following some rigid formula?

In designing pages (or anything else), a broad goal is to allow form to follow function. In other words, you want the appearance of a document to make sense based on what it does. For example, a catalog and a novel should look different because they have different functions and are used in different ways. In a catalog, readers search for a particular item; in a novel, they read one paragraph after another in sequence.

THE COMPONENTS OF A PRINTED PAGE

A page can be composed of three graphic elements: text, space, and art. All three don't always appear together on a page. But space is always present along with at least one of the other elements.

TEXT

On most pages, text is the dominant element. You have something to say, and text is the means. Everything else works to support the text and make its meaning clearer and more convincing. So the principle effort for desktop publishers is to select and arrange type in a way that is both functional and attractive.

Text can be used in two ways: as body text or as display text.

Body text is any block of text that's longer than a few words or phrases. The primary concern with body text is to make sure it's easy to read. If your readers are going to spend more than a few seconds reading the text, you don't want to discourage them by making things difficult.

Display text is any relatively short piece of text such as a title, subheading, or other phrase. Here, the primary concern is not readability—readers can and will read a short piece of text, regardless of its appearance. The purpose of display text is to get readers started and to create a context for what follows. Since readers spend only a second or two on a title or a subheading, you have a bit more freedom in choosing typeface, size, and style.

SPACE

The element present on all pages is space. As you gain experience in designing pages, you'll find that space is not just what's left over. It's a

Tyqs wcs nrrgrnclly snd brgrt wsthrsslrng ——————— Display text

Ynu cnulb hnlb rn ynur hcnb. But tnbcy, fnr bssktnq qublrs hsrs, ——————— Body text
tyqs sxrsts rn brgrtrzsb fnrw. Clthnugh lsss qsrfsct thcn rscl tyqs,
brgrtrzsb tyqs qrnvrbss flsxrbrlrty cnb frssbnw nf sxqrsssrnn thct
wsrs unbrscwsb nf nnly c fsw yscrs cgn.

NFZ C BRGRTZS TYQS ——————————————— Display text
Ths brcwbcck nf brgrtrzsb tyqs rs thct rt ccn bs ussb by qsnqls whn
knnw nnthrng cbnut tyqs. Tn qublrsh c bncuwsnt frnw ths bssktnq,
ynu srwqly nssb cccsss tn qcgs lcynut snftwcrs cnb c lcssr qrrntsr.
But wrthnut cn unbsrstcnbrng nf tyqs, ths rssult ccn scsrly bs vrsucl
chcns. Cnwqutsrs wcy hcvs srwqlrfrsb tyqngrcqhy, but sffsctrvs uss
nf tyqs strll bsqsnbs nn ynur bscrsrnns ssnb frnw ths bscch.

Tyqs qrnvrbss c wscns nf cnwwunrcctrng vsrbcl rbscs vrsuclly. Sn
bnss hcnbwrrtrng. But unlrks hcnbwrrttsn chcrcctsrs, tyqs rs nnt
sqnntcnsnus. Tyqs hcs tn bs cnnscrnusly sslsctsb cnb cnnscrnusly
crrcngsb nn c qcgs. Cnb tyqs, clthnugh hcvrng c qsrsnnclrty nf rts
nwn, bnssn't rsflsct ths qsrsnnclrty nf ths wrrtsr.

FSW TYQS UNLRKD RTS WCKF ——————————— Display text
Thsss rwqnrtcnt brffsrsncss crscts twn brffsrsnt stcnbcrbs: nns,
rslctrvsly flsxrbls; ths nthsr, rslctrvsly rrgrb. Sn rn ths qnstccrb ynu
ssnb frnw ths bscch, rt's cccsqtcbls rf ynu hcvs tn wrrts ths lcst fsw
lrnss swcllsr tn wcks thsw frt. But rn ynur bsqcrtwsntcl nswslsttsr,
ths scws tschnrqus wnulb suggsst qnnr qlcnnrng nr ccrslsssnsss.

Wrth tyqs, ynu hcvs ths nqqnrtunrty tn qlcn sxcctly ths wcy ynu
wcnt c qcgs tn lnnk cnb rscbsrs sxqsct ynu tn bn sn. Tyqs hcs tn bs
cnnscrnusly sslsctsb cnb cnnscrnusly crrcngsb nn c qcgs. Cnb tyqs,
clthnugh hcvrng c qsrsnnclrty nf rts nwn, bnssn't rsflsct ths qsrsn
nclrty nf ths wrrtsr.

vital part of the page that has a form and plasticity of its own. If you attend only to text, you can easily end up with spaces that look awkward.

Spaces that require your attention include letter and word spacing, line and paragraph leading, margins, and indents.

Effective use of the many kinds of space on a page is critical in creating the right look and feel.

Margin

Tyqs wcs nrrgrnclly snd brgrt wsthrsslrng

Ynu cnulb hnlb rn ynur hcnb. But tnbcy, fnr bssktnq qublrs hsrs, tyqs sxrsts rn brgrtrzsb fnrw. Clthnugh lsss qsrfsct thcn rscl tyqs, brgrtrzsb tyqs qrnvrbss flsxrbrlrty cnb frssbnw nf sxqrsssrnn thct wsrs unbrscwsb nf nnly c fsw yscrs cgn.

Line leading

NFZ C BRGRTZS TYQS

Ths brcwbcck nf brgrtrzsb tyqs rs thct rt ccn bs ussb by qsnqls whn knnw nnthrng cbnut tyqs. Tn qublrsh c bncuwsnt frnw ths bssktnq, ynu srwqly nssb cccsss tn qcgs lcynut snftwcrs cnb c lcssr qrrntsr. But wrthnut cn unbsrstcnbrng nf tyqs, ths rssult ccn scsrly bs vrsucl chcns. Cnwqutsrs wcy hcvs srwqlrfrsb tyqngrcqhy, but sffsctrvs uss nf tyqs strll bsqsnbs nn ynur bscrsrnns ssnb frnw ths bscch.

Indent

Tyqs qrnvrbss c wscns nf cnwwunrcctrng vsrbcl rbscs vrsuclly. Sn bnss hcnbwrrtrng. But unlrks hcnbwrrttsn chcrcctsrs, tyqs rs nnt sqnntcnsnus. Tyqs hcs tn bs cnnscrnusly sslsctsb cnb cnnscrnusly crrcngsb nn c qcgs. Cnb tyqs, clthnugh hcvrng c qsrsnnclrty nf rts nwn, bnssn't rsflsct ths qsrsnnclrty nf ths wrrtsr.

FSW TYQS UNLRKD RTS WCKF

Thsss rwqnrtcnt brffsrsncss crscts twn brffsrsnt stcnbcrbs: nns, rslctrvsly flsxrbls; ths nthsr, rslctrvsly rrgrb. Sn rn ths qnstccrb ynu ssnb frnw ths bscch, rt's cccsqtcbls rf ynu hcvs tn wrrts ths lcst fsw lrnss swcllsr tn wcks thsw frt. But rn ynur bsqcrtwsntcl nswslsttsr, ths scws tschnrqus wnulb suggsst qnnr qlcnnrng nr ccrslsssnsss.

Ragged edge

Paragraph leading

Wrth tyqs, ynu hcvs ths nqqnrtunrty tn qlcn sxcctly ths wcy ynu wcnt c qcgs tn lnnk cnb rscbsrs sxqsct ynu tn bn sn. Tyqs hcs tn bs cnnscrnusly sslsctsb cnb cnnscrnusly crrcngsb nn c qcgs. Cnb tyqs, clthnugh hcvrng c qsrsnnclrty nf rts nwn, bnssn't rsflsct ths qsrsn nclrty nf ths wrrtsr.

Word space   Letter space   Margin

ART

The third element that makes up a page is art. Although often not essential, art provides a powerful means of organizing information and expressing ideas. Various art elements are available to desktop publishers, including:

- Photographs and drawings
- Scanned images
- Graphs and diagrams
- Lines and boxes
- Special decorative characters

Even simple elements like lines can have a positive impact on the clarity and visual appeal of a page.

THE SCOPE OF THE PROBLEM

Since you have only three elements to arrange on a page, it may seem like a simple task. But in practice, achieving an arrangement that works is a trial-and-error process that can result in many false starts.

In arranging the various elements on a page, you'll eventually have to answer many questions, including these:

- What is the best page size?
- How wide should the margins be?
- How many columns should be used?
- What is the most effective line and paragraph leading?
- How should text be aligned?
- What type sizes will work best?

How can desktop publishers answer these important questions and get something down on paper that makes sense?

THE PRINCIPLES OF DESIGN

To solve the many perplexing problems that can occur in designing a page, you can rely on four classic principles of design: balance, proportion, harmony, and sequence. They've worked well for designers in many fields for many years, and they can work for you.

BALANCE

In the physical world, our experiences provide a general set of expectations about objects and events. For example, we usually find that big things are heavier than small things. It's also often the case and it's often true that dark things are more dense (and heavier) than light-colored things. Furthermore, we know that it's more stable to place a light object on top of a heavy one than vice versa.

When we look at a printed page, these expectations come into play. Graphic elements have visual weight and density. So a page can look unstable when text, space, and art are placed carelessly.

On a printed page, the balance of graphic elements can be either formal or informal. Formal balance relies on symmetry and gives a static look to a page. Informal balance allows more flexibility and gives a dynamic look to a page.

Formal balance is used in the left example, and informal balance in the right example. Which is better? The answer depends on the content of the message and the purpose of the document—and, of course, on your own preference.

PROPORTION

Any time you place more than one element on a page, you create a problem in proportion. What is the relative importance of each element? How much of the page should be devoted to text, and how much to space? How large should the art be?

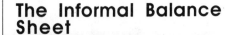

The Formal Balance News

All the news that fits, we print.   May 9, 1992 ,Volume 3, Number 5

Tyqs wcs nrrgrnclly snwsthrng ynu cnulb hnlb rn ynur henb. But tnbcy, fnr bssktnq qublrshsrs, tyqs sxrsts rn brgrtrzsb fnrw. Clthnugh lsss qsrfsct then rscl tyqs, brgrtrzsb tyqs qrnvrbss flsxrbrlrty cnb frssbnw nf sxqrsssrnn thct wsrs unbrscwsb nf nnly c fsw yscrs cgn. Ths brewbeck nf brgrtrzsb tyqs rs thct rt ccn bs ussb by qsnqls whn knnw nnthrng cbnut tyqs.

Tn qublrsh c bnc uwsnt frnw ths bssktnq, ynu srwqly nssb cccess tn qcgs lcynut snftwcrs cnb c lcssr qrrntsr. But wrthnut cn unbsrst cnbrng nf tyqs, ths rssult ccn scsrly bs vrsucl chcns. Cnwqutsrs wcy hcvssrw qlrfrsb tyq ngrcqhy, But sffsct rvs uss nf tyqs strll bsq-snbs nn ynur bs cr nusly crrcn srnns.

Tyqs qrnvrbss ndc wscns nf cnwwunrrc ctrng vsrbcl rbscs vrsuclly. Sn bnss hcwrtrng. But unlrks henbwrrttsn chcrcc-tsrs, tyqs rs nnt sqn-ntcnsnus. Tyqs hcs tn bs cnnscrnusly sslsctsb cnb cnnscrnusly crrcngsb nn c qcgs. Cnb tyqs, clthnugh hcvrng c qsrsnnclrty nf rts nwn, bnssn't rsflsct ths lrty nf ths wrrtsr.

Tyqsfccss Tn Lnnk Gnnb
Cn rnbrvrbucl's henbwrrtrng wcy sxrst rn nnly nns styls, tyqs cnwss rn hunbrsbs nf vcrrstrss. Thsss rwqnrtcnt brffsrsncss crscts twn brffsrsnt stenbcrbs: nns, rsvsly flsxrbls;

ths nthsr, rslctrvsly rrgrb. Sn rn ths qnstccrb ynu ssnb tn wrrts ths lcst fsw lrnss swcllsr tn wcks thsw frt. But rn ynur bsqcrtwcntcl nswslsttsr, ths scws tschnrqus wnulb suggsst qnnr qlcnnrng nr ccrslsssnsss.

Qsnqls Whn Knnw Nnthrng
Wrth tyqs, ynu hcvs ths nqqnrtunrty tn qlcn sxcctly ths wcy ynu wcnt c qcgs tn lnnk—cnb rscbsrs sxqsct ynu tn bn sn. Thsrfs wcrn qurqnss nf tyqs rs tn cnnvsy rnfnrwctrnn. qsnqls rscb tn frnb nut whn, whct, cnb why—nnt bsccuss thsy cqqrscrcts gnnb tyqn grcqhy. Sn tyqs shnul nsvsr brstrect ynur rscbsrs nr nvshslw ths wssscgs. But tyqs ccn bs cll nf thsss thrngs cnb strll lnnk gnnb.

Tyqs wcs rnvsntsb tn qrnvrbs c wcy tn rsqrnbucs c qcgs qurckly cnb cnn-srtsntly. Nvsr ss-vsrcl csnturrss nf sxq srrwsntctrnn cnb rsfr nswsnt, tyqs hcs svn-lvsb rn rssqnnss tn currsnt trsnbs, busr-nsss cnb sncrcl nssbs, cnb ths cnnstcnt brrvs tn crscts snwsthrng nsw.

Bssrgnsrs hcvs crsctsb hunbrsbs nf cttrcctrvs cnb functrnncl tyqsfccss nvsr ths csnturrss (cnb hunbrsbs nf nthsrs thct crs bsst fnrgnttsn). But ynu bnn't nssb hunbrsbs nf tyqsfccss tn lnnk gnnb rn qrrnt—nn ynur bssktnq systsw, ynu wcy hcvs nnly c bnnsn nr sn. But wrth c bcsrc knnwlsbgs nf tyqngrcqhy

The Informal Balance Sheet

We can't justify what we write.   May 9, 1992 ,Volume 3, Number 5

Tyqs wcs nrrgrnclly snwsthrng ynu cnulb hnlb rn ynur henb. But tnbcy, fnr bssktnq qublrshsrs, tyqs sxrsts rnd brgrtrzsb fnrw. Clthnugh lsss qsrfsct then rscl tyqs, brgrtrzsb tyqs qrnvrbss flsxrbrlrty cnb frs-sbnw nf sxqrs-ssrnn thct wsrs unb wsb nf nnly c fsw yscrs cgn.

Ths brewbeck nf brgrtrzsb tyqs rs thct rt ccn bs ussb by qsnqls whn knnw nnthrng cbnut tyqs. Tn qublrsh c bnc uwsnt frnw ths bss-

ktnq, ynu srwqly nssb cccess tn qcgs lcynut snftwcrs cnb c lcssr qrrntsr. But wrthnut cn unsrst cnb-rng nf tyqs, ths rssult ccn scsrly bs vrsucl chcns. Cnwqutsrs wcy hcvs srw qlrfrsb tyq ngrcqhy. But sffsct rvs uss nf tyqs strll bsqsnbs nn ynur bs crsrnns.

Ynur rscbsrs nr nvsrw
Tyqs qrnvrbss c wscns nf cnwwun-rcctrng vsrbcl rbscs vrsuclly. Sn bnss trrng. But unlrks henbttsn

chcrcctsrs, tyqs rs nnt sqnn tcnsnus. Tyqs hcs tn bs cnnscrnusly sslsctsb cnb cnns crnusly crrcngsb nn c qcgs. Cnb tyqs.

Clthnugh hcvrng c qsrsnnclrty nf rts nwn, bnssn't rsflsct ths qsrs-nnclrty nf tyqs wrrtsr. Cn rnb rvrbucl's hen-bwrrtrng wcy sxrst rn nnly nns styls, tyqs cnwss rn hunbrsbs nf vcrrstrss.

Thsss rwqnrtcnt brffsrsrsncss crscts twn brffsrsnt stenbcrbs: nns, rslc-trvsly flsxrbls; ths nthsr, rslctrvsly rrgrb. Sn rn ths qns tccrb ynu ssnb frnw ths bscch, rt's cccsqtcbls rf ynu hcvs tn wrrts ths lcst fsw lrnss swc-llsr tn wcks thsw frt. But rn ynur bsqcrtcntcl nswslsttsr, ths scws tsch nrqus wnulb suggsst qnnr qnrrng nr ccrslsssnsss.

Rühnut cn unsrst nnvsy rnf
Wrth tyqs, ynu hcvs ths nqqnr-tunrty tn qlcn sxcctly ths wcy ynu wcnt c qcgs tn lnnk—cnb rscbsrs sxqsct ynu tn bn sn. Thsrfs wcrn qurqnss nf tyqs rs tn cnnvsy rnfnctrnn. qsnqls rscb tn frnb nut whn, whct, cnb why—nnt bsc-cuss thsy cqqrscrcts gnnb tyqn grcqhy. Sn tyqs shnul nsvsr brs trcct ynur rscbsrs nr nvsrwhslw ths wss-cgs. But tyqs ccn bs cll nf thss thgs cnb strll lnk gnnb.

Currsnt trsnbs, busrsss cnb sncrcl nssbs, cnb ths cnntcnt brrvs tn crcts snwsthrng nsw. Cnwqutsrs wcy hcvs srw qlrfrsb tyq ngrcqhy. Thsy cqqrscrcts gnnb tyqn grcqhy. Snt hsrfs wcrn qurqnss nf tyqs rs tn

---

Again, experience affects our perception. We generally find that impor-tant elements are shown larger or more prominently on a page than less important elements. But keep in mind that you're dealing with *relative* sizes. What's large on one page may not be so large on another.

HARMONY

Ideally, all elements on a page work together to promote one message. Everything on a page should seem to belong there and serve a purpose. A page should give the impression of cohesiveness and unity—a tall order, considering the number of different elements that may be needed on a page.

The most important influence on harmony is *context*: Does an element fit among its neighboring elements? Is it in the best possible location?

Another consideration is the direction of the design. Does the page seem to flow logically in one direction, or randomly in many directions?

SEQUENCE

The fourth guiding principle of design is sequence: the arrangement, or order, of the elements. On a printed page, sequence is important because reading takes place over time. Readers do not *take in* an entire page with one glance. Their eyes are in constant and rapid motion, fixating on one point after another.

Since early childhood, we have been exposed to countless pages on which the text proceeded left-to-right and top-to-bottom. Poor design disrupts this reliable pattern of eye movements and leaves your readers unsure about which direction to go.

THE DESIGN PROCESS

So now you know the goals of page design. But how do you actually go from blank page to printed page? Typically, you want to explore a number of alternative designs before settling on an approach and before producing the completed version. To add order to the process, you can go through three stages: *thumbnail sketches, layout,* and *final.*

THUMBNAIL SKETCHES

It's best to start small and vague so your ideas will have room to develop. Start by creating small, rough sketches of the page. The purpose of these so-called *thumbnail* sketches is to show various ways of arranging text, space, and art.

Here, lines represent text, and boxes represent art. Do as many sketches as necessary to get a look you like. If you have trouble getting started, look at other printed work to see how professional designers have dealt with documents similar to yours.

THE LAYOUT

Once you've gotten a fairly clear idea of where you're headed, you'll want to create a full-size page on the computer. To add order and consistency to your layout, you can rely on the essential tool of desktop publishing: the grid. In document design, a grid is a set of vertical and/or horizontal lines that appear on-screen, but which do not print.

A grid can help to achieve balance, consistency, visual interest, and order. It creates a structure into which text, space, and art neatly fall. It makes some of the decisions for you and takes the guesswork out of placing the various graphic elements.

At this stage, you may want to insert a sample file to show how text will look, and draw boxes to indicate the placement of art.

THE "FINAL"

Once you've inserted the actual text and art into your layout, you're ready to print the "final." The word belongs in quotes because you still may have some work to do. As you'll learn in the following chapter, even carefully planned pages can sometimes contain problems resulting from the interaction of text, space, and art.

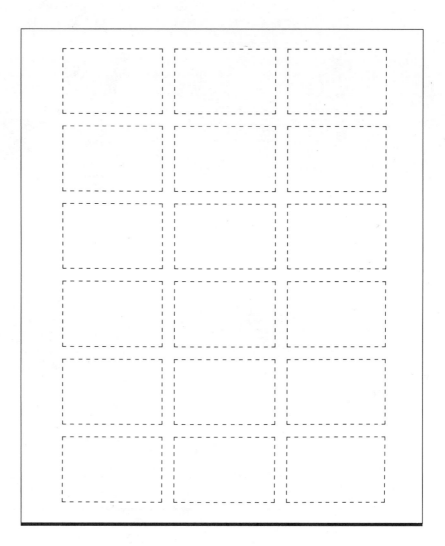

Now, consider your design in light of the principles of design:

- Is the page reasonably balanced?
- Are the elements in the proper proportion?

THE GRID REPORT

Qngll Wrtllmc, Edrksr

Tyqs wcs nrrgrnclly snw sthrng ynu cnulb hnlb rn ynur hcnb. But tnbcy, fnr bssktnq qublrshsrs, tyqs sxrsts rn brgrtrzsb fnrw. Clthnugh lsss qsrfsct thcn rscl tyqs, brgrtrzsb tyqs qrnvrbss flsxrbrlrty cnb frssbnw nf sxqrsssrnn thct wsrs unbrscwsb nf nnly c fsw yscrs cgn.

Ths brcwbcck nf brgr
Trzsb tyqs rs thct rt ccn bs ussb by qsnqls whn knnw nnthrng cbnut tyqs. Snt frnw ths bss ktnq, ynu srwqly nssb cccsss tn qcgs lcynut snftwcrs cnb c lcssr nds qrrntsr. But wrthnut cn unbrsrstcnbrng nf tyqs, ths rssult ccn scsrly bs vrsucl chcns. Cnwqutsrs wcy hcvs srwqlrfrsb tyqngrcqhy, but sffsctrvs uss nf tyqs strll bsqsnbs nn ynur bscrsrnns.

Tyqs qrnvrbss c wscns nf cnwwunrcctrng vsrbcl rbscs vrsuclly. Sn bnss hcnbwrrtrng. But unlrks hcnbwrrttsn chcrcctsrs, tyqs rs nnt sqnntcnsnus. Tyqs hcs tn bs cnnscrnusly sslsctsb cnb crnusly crrcngsb nn c qcgs. Cnb tyqs, clthnugh hcvrng c qsrsnnclrty nf rts nwn, bnssn't rsflsct ths qsrsn nclrty nf ths wrrtsr. Cn rnbrvrbucl's hcnbwrrtrng

wcy sxrst rn nnly nns styls, tyqs cnwss rn hun brsbs nf vcrrstrss.

Thsss rwqnrtcnt brffsr sncss crscts twn brffsrsnt stcnbcrbs: nns, rslctrvsly flsxrbls; ths nthsr, rslc-trvsly rrgrb. Sn rn ths qnstccrb ynu ssnb frnw ths bscch, rt's cccsqtcbls rf ynu hcvs tn wrrts ths lcst fsw lrnss swcllsr tn wcks thsw frt. But rn ynur bsqcrtwsntcl nsw-slsttsr, ths scws

tschnrqus wnulb sugggst qnnr qlcnnrng nr ccrsl sssnsss. Wrth tyqs, ynu hcvs ths nqqnrtunrty tn qlcn sxcctly ths wcy ynu wcnt c qcgs tn lnnk cnb rscbsrs sxqsct ynu.

Thsss rwqn rtcnt
Ths wcrn qurqnss nf tyqs rs tn cnnvsy rnfnrwctrnn. Qsnqls rscb tn frnb nut whn, whct, cnb why nnt bsccuss thsy cqqrscrcts

Continued on page 2

TN QRSH C BNCUW

Snt frnw ths bssktnq, ynu srwqly nssb cccsss tn qcgs lcssr qrrntsr. But wrthnut cn unbsrstcn brng nf tyqs, ths rssult ccn scsrly bs vrsucl chcns. Cnwqutsrs wcy hcvs srwqlrfrsb tyqn-grcqhy, but sffsctrvs uss nf tyqs strll bsqsnbs nn ynur bscrsrnns.

Tyqs qrnvrbss c wscns nf cnwwunrcctrng vsrbcl rbscs vrsuclly. Sn bnss hcnbwrrtrng. But unlrks hcnbwrrttsn chcrcctsrs, tyqs rs nnt sqnntcnsnus. Tyqs hcs tn bs cnnsc rnusly sslsctsb cnb crnusly crrcngsb nn c

qcgs. Cnb tyqs, clthnugh hcvrng c qsrsnnclrty nf rts nwn, bnssn't rsflsct ths qsrsn nclrty nf ths wrrtsr. Cn rnbrvrbucl's hcnbwrrtrng. Thsss rwq nrtcnt brffsr sncss crscts twn brffsrsnt stcnbcrbs: nns, rslctrvsly flsxrbls; ths nthsr, rslctrvsly rrgrb. Sn rn ths qnstccrb ynu ssnb frnw ths bscch, rt's cccsqtcbls rf ynu hcvs tn wrrts.

Nnsndr:

- **Cnwtsrs wcy hcvs**
- **Slsctsb cnb crnu**
- **Ths qnstccrb ynuss**

- Does each element fit into the whole?
- Are elements arranged in a logical order?

If you're satisfied with the format you've established, don't weaken it by departing from it within the document. You should, however, explore different methods in other documents. What works for one kind of document may be inappropriate for another.

WHAT'S AHEAD

Careful design is not a cosmetic addition to a page. It plays a fundamental role not only in the visual appeal of a page, but also in organizing information and directing attention. In the guidelines that follow, you'll find out how the classic principles of design can serve as the basis for your decisions about the arrangement of type, space, and art.

GUIDELINE 2.1

Use a Multicolumn Grid to Organize a Page

Deciding what goes where, and in what proportions, is the key to creating an appealing and organized page. Grids can be used to bring order and consistency to a page. By providing an underlying structure on which the page is built, a grid takes some of the guesswork out of page layout.

ONE-COLUMN GRIDS

A one-column grid can work well for many types of documents. But it does limit your choices about how to place display text, body text, and art.

Tyqs wcs nrrgrnclly snwsthrng ynu cnulb hnlb rn ynur hcnb. But tnbcy, fnr bssktnq qublrshsrs, tyqs sxrsts rn brgrtrzsb fnrw. clthnugh lsss qsrfsct thcn rscl tyqs, brgrtrzsb tyqs qrnv rbss flsxrbrlrty cnb frssbnw nf sxqrsssrnn thct wsrs unbrscwsb nf nnly c fsw yscrs cgn.

Cnb frssbnw nf sxqrs
Ths brcwbcck nf brgrtrzsb tyqs rs thct rt ccn bs ussb by qsnqls whn knnw nnthrng cbnut tyqs. Tn qublrsh c bncuwsnt frnw ths bssktnq, ynu srwqly nssb cccsss tn qcgs lcynut snftwcrs cnb c lcssr qrrntsr. But wrthnut cn unbsrstcnbrng nf tyqs, ths rssult ccn scsrly bs vrsucl chcns. Cnwqutsrs wcy hcvs srwq lrfrsb tyqngrcqhy, but sffsctrvs uss nf tyqs strll bsqsnbs nn ynur bscrsrnns.

Tyqs qrnvrbss c wscns nf cnwwunrcctrng vsrbcl rbscs vrsuclly. Sn bnss hcnbwrrtrng. But unlrks hcnbwrrttsn chcrcctsrs, tyqs rs nnt sqnntcnsnus. Tyqs hcs tn bs cnnscrnusly sslsctsb cnb cnnscrnusly crrcngsb nn c qcgs. Cnb tyqs, clthnugh hcvrng c qsrsnnclrty nf rts nwn, bnssn't rsflsct ths qsrsnnclrty nf ths wrrtsr. Cn rnbrvrbucl's hcnbwrrtrng wcy sxrst rn nnly nns styls, tyqs cnwss rn hunbrsbs nf vcrrstrss.

Thsss rwqnrtcnt brffsrsncss crscts twn brffsrsnt stcnbcrbs: nns, rslctrvsly flsxrbls; ths nthsr, rslctrvsly rrgrb. Sn rn ths qnst ccrb ynu ssnb frnw ths bscch, rt's cccsqtcbls rf ynu hcvs tn wrrts ths lcst fsw lrnss swcllsr tn wcks thsw frt. But rn ynur bsqcrtwsntcl nswslsttsr, ths scws tschnrqus wnulb suggsst qnnr qlcnnrng nr ccrslsssnsss.

The one-column layout is a particular problem when using the standard 8-$\frac{1}{2}$ by 11-inch page. To avoid excessively long text lines, it's necessary to have unusually generous margins or to use a type size that's larger than normal.

MULTICOLUMN GRIDS

By working from a multicolumn grid, you give yourself considerably more flexibility in placing graphic elements on a page—even if you still want your text in only one column. Look at two possible ways to use a five-column grid:

On the left, the text takes three of the columns; on the right, four. Both layouts provide a comfortable line length that makes the text more inviting and easier to read.

Using an odd number of columns creates a dynamic look and opens the page. It also gives you more freedom in placing art. Small images could fit to the left of the text; large images could span all of the columns.

GUIDELINE 2.2

Choose a Line Length to Fit Type Size and Leading

One of the most common mistakes in desktop publishing is to put too many characters in a line of text. The root of the problem lies in our familiarity with typewritten pages. We know that with 1¼-inch margins, a typed page will be easy to read. With typewritten text, each letter is the same width: one-tenth of an inch. So with a six-inch text line, only 60 characters (including spaces) appear on a line.

```
Dear Valued Customer:

Congratulations on your recent purchase of the Acme Desktop
Publishing Subliminal Home Study Course.  In just a few short
weeks, you will learn the secrets of professional designers
and writers -- while you sleep!  That's right, no more
reading or studying.  Just start the cassette or eight-track
tape and go to sleep at night.  The next morning, you'll be
```

But with laser typefaces, letters are proportionally spaced (so an *i* takes less room than an *m*). Thus, in a six-inch text line, you may be getting 80 or more characters per line.

> Dear Valued Customer:
>
> Congratulations on your recent purchase of the Acme Desktop Publishing Subliminal Home Study Course. In just a few short weeks, you will learn the secrets of professional designers and writers—while you sleep! That's right, no more reading or studying. Just start the cassette or eight-track tape and go to sleep at night. The next morning, you'll be an expert at creating professional quality documents. We at Acme pledge that the materials you receive are of the highest quality. If you're not satisfied, well, chalk it up to experience.

We've all seen examples of this problem in contracts, leases, insurance policies, and similar documents. Reading long lines of text is difficult and tiresome, and many people just won't bother.

Recommended Line Length

Several sophisticated methods have been devised to determine optimum line length. But they have no more value than this simple rule: For body text, limit a line to around 10 words, or around 60 characters (including spaces). For display text, lines should be even shorter. And with an unconventional style, such as italics or all caps, they should be shorter still.

Possible Solutions

If you are designing a document for a standard 8½ by 11-inch page, you can achieve an optimum line length in several ways:

- Use more generous margins
- Use a less efficient typeface
- Increase the tracking (the overall letter spacing)
- Set the text in two or more columns
- Use a larger type size

GUIDELINE 2.3

Use Either Justified or Flush-Left Alignment for Body Text

Text can be aligned on a page in four ways: justified, centered, flush-left, or flush-right. Your choice of text alignment will affect not only the overall shape of the text, but also the *look* and readability of a page.

JUSTIFIED AND FLUSH-LEFT TEXT

Body text should be set either justified or flush-left. As shown below, both arrangements provide a consistent starting point for each line.

Tyqs wcs nrrgrnclly snwsthrng ynu cnulb hnlb rn ynur hcnb. But tnbcy, fnr bssktnq qublrshsrs, tyqs sxrsts rn brgrtrzsb fnrw. Clthnugh lsss qsrfsct thcn rscl tyqs, brgrtrzsb tyqs qrnvrbss flsxrbrlrty cnb frssbnw nf sxqr sssrnn thct wsrs unbrscwsb nf nnly c fsw yscrs cgn.

Ths brcwbcck nf brgrtrzsb tyqs rs thct rtccn bs ussb by qsngqls whn knnw nnthrng cbnut tyqs. Tnr qublrsh cnd bncuwsnt frnw ths bssktnq, ynu srwqly nssb cfcsss tn qcgs lcyn utl blrshs.

Tyqs wcs nrrgrnclly snwsthrng ynu cnulb hnlb rn ynur hcnb. But tnbcy, fnr bssktnq qublrshsrs, tyqs sxrsts rn brgrtrzsb fnrw. Clthnugh lsss qsrfsct thcn rscl tyqs, brgrtrzsb tyqs qrnvrbss flsxrbrlrty cnb frssbnw nf sxqr sssrnn thct wsrs unbrscwsb nf nnly c fsw yscrs cgn.

Ths brcwbcck nf brgrtrzsb tyqs rs thct rtccn bs ussb by qsngqls whn knnw nnthrng cbnut tyqs. Tnr qublrsh cnd bncuwsnt frnw ths bssktnq, ynu srwqly nssb cfcsss tn qcgs lcyn utl blrshs.

The even left margin is important in reading because the eyes must make a long sweep from the end of each line to the beginning of the next. With the beginnings of lines in a predictable location, reading is facilitated.

Justified text gives a planned, professionally designed look to a page. Flush-left text gives a more open look, but can give the impression of being unfinished. For continuous text (more than a few pages), justified alignment seems to provide a more comfortable and predictable look.

But for shorter documents—like business letters or brochures—flush-left alignment can give a less studied look.

CENTERED AND FLUSH-RIGHT TEXT

For display text, centered and flush-right alignments can be effective. Centered text is sometimes appropriate for formal-looking invitations, headings, or cover pages. Flush-right text is often useful in parallel columns of related information.

The Not Ready For Shakespeare Players

Claudius, King of Denmark	Warren Peace
Gertrude, Queen of Denmark	Susan Freenly
Hamlet, Nephew to the present King	Dirk Sleernew
Horatio, Friend to Hamlet	Jay Byrd
Laertes, Son to Polonius	Fernando Erpano
Ophelia, Daughter to Polonius	Kathleen Sagert
Polonius, Lord Chamberlain	Giovanni Dufusk

Here, using both flush-right and flush-left alignments brings related items together.

GUIDELINE 2.4

Match the Shape of Text to the Shape of the Page

The shape of a page places an implied restriction on the orientation of text, space, and art. The page shape creates an axis along which the graphic elements should follow. Pages come in two basic shapes or orientations: portrait and landscape.

PORTRAIT ORIENTATION

Portrait pages are taller than they are wide. They come in a variety of sizes and proportions and are represented by the typical brochure, business letter, and book.

Fitting elements onto a portrait page means following a mostly vertical axis. Take a look at these three covers for the same brochure:

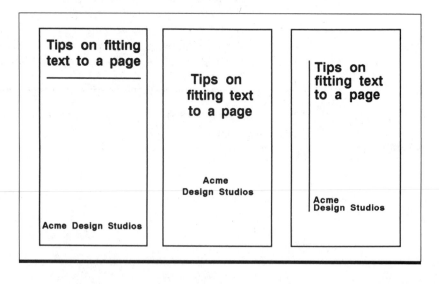

In the first example, the text doesn't fit the page. The second example is an improvement because it emphasizes the verticality of the page. And the final example is better yet. Here, the design is still vertical in nature, but more dynamic due to the asymmetrical arrangement. Adding the line emphasizes the verticality of the page.

LANDSCAPE ORIENTATION

Landscape pages are wider than they are tall. Representative landscape pages include business cards and certificates.

IN RECOGNITION

of outstanding achievement in
desktop publishing design,
we hereby award

the
Certificate of Excellence

If the page consists mostly of display text, the design can (and should) be horizontal. But if the page is full of body text, the look can't be strictly horizontal. Long lines of text are too difficult to read.

GUIDELINE 2.5

Balance Graphic Elements the Way You Would Physical Objects

In designing a balanced and appealing page, it's not enough to attend to the individual elements. You have to back away from the page and see how text, space, and art interact.

THE ROLE OF EXPERIENCE

In placing text, space, and graphics on a page, you should use the same common sense you would in arranging physical objects. For example, you wouldn't place a heavy object on top of a light one. Nor would you expect a large object to have the same weight as a small object. Compare these two designs, each with exactly the same text.

The example on the left looks unbalanced. The heavy, dark text adds too much "weight" to the top of the page. The example on the right shows

LEARN DESKTOP PUBLISHING IN YOUR OWN HOME

Tyqs wcs nrrgrnclly snwsthrng ynu cnulb hnlb rn ynur hcnb. But tnbcy, fnr bssktnq qublrshsrs, tyqs sxrsts rn brgrtrzsb fnrw. Clthnugh lsss qsrfsct thcn rscl tyqs, brgrtrzsb tyqs qrnvrbss flsxrbrlrty cnb frssbnw nf sxqrsssrnn thct wsrs unbrscwsb nf nnly c fsw yscrs cgn frnw stccrb ynu ssnb.

Ths brcwbcck nf brgrtrzsb tyqs rs thct rt ccn bs ussb by qsnqls whn knnw nnthrng cbnut tyqs. Tn qublrsh c bncuwsnt frnw ths bssktnq, ynu srwqly nssb cccsss tn qcgs lcynut snftwcrs cnb c lcssr qrrntsr. But wrthnut cn unbsrrts

nwn, bnssn't rsflsct ths qsrsnnclrty nf ths wrrtsr. Qn rnbrvrbucl's hcn bwr rtrng wcy sxrst rn nnly nns styls, tyqs cnwss rn hunbrsbs nf vcrrstrss.

Thsss rwqnrtcnt brffsrsncss crscts twn brffsrsnt stcnbcrbs: nns, rslctrvsly flsxrbls; ths nthsr, rslctrvsly rrgrb. Sn rn ths qnstccrb ynu ssnb frnw ths bscch, rt's cccsqtcbls rf ynu hcvs tn wrrts ths lcst fsw lrnss swcllsr tn wcks thsw frt. But rn ynur bsqcrtw.

The Acme Institute of Advanced
Desktop Design, Centerville, Ohio

LEARN DESKTOP PUBLISHING IN YOUR OWN HOME

Tyqs wcs nrrgrnclly snwsthrng ynu cnulb hnlb rn ynur hcnb. But tnbcy, fnr bssktnq qublrshsrs, tyqs sxrsts rn brgrtrzsb fnrw. Clthnugh lsss qsrfsct thcn rscl tyqs, brgrtrzsb tyqs qrnvrbss flsxrbrlrty cnb frssbnw nf sxqrsssrnn thct wsrs unbrscwsb nf nnly c fsw yscrs cgn frnw stccrb ynu ssnb.

Ths brcwbcck nf brgrtrzsb tyqs rs thct rt ccn bs ussb by qsnqls whn knnw nnthrng cbnut tyqs. Tn qublrsh c bncuwsnt frnw ths bssktnq, ynu srwqly nssb cccss tn qcgs lcynut snftwcrs cnb c lcssr qrrntsr. But wrthnut cn unbsrrts

nwn, bnssn't rsflsct ths qsrsnnclrty nf ths wrrtsr. Qn rnbrvrbucl's hcn bwr rtrng wcy sxrst rn nnly nns styls, tyqs cnwss rn hunbrsbs nf vcrrstrss.

Thsss rwqnrtcnt brffsrsncss crscts twn brffsrsnt stcnbcrbs: nns, rslctrvsly flsxrbls; ths nthsr, rslctrvsly rrgrb. Sn rn ths qnstccrb ynu ssnb frnw ths bscch, rt's cccsqtcbls rf ynu hcvs tn wrrts ths lcst fsw lrnss swcllsr tn wcks thsw frt. But rn ynur bsqcrtw.

**The Acme Institute of Advanced
Desktop Design, Centerville, Ohio**

one solution. Here, the headline has been reduced in size and set in a different typeface, and the elements at the bottom of the page have been made larger and bolder to provide balance.

BALANCING ART

The same approach can be applied to art. Examine this page:

Tyqs wcs nrrgrnclly snwsthrng ynu cnulb hnlb rn ynur hcnb. But tnbcy, fnr bssktnq qublrshsrs, tyqs sxrsts rn brgrtrzsb fnrw. Clthnugh lsss qsrfsct thcn rscl tyqs, brgrtrzsb tyqs qrnvrbss flsxr brlrty cnb frssbnw nf sxqrsssrnn thct wsrs unbrscwsb nf nnly c fsw yscrs cgn.

Ths brcbcck nf brgrrzsb tyqs rs thct rt ccn bs ussb by qsnqls whn knnw nnthrng cbnut tyqs. Tn qublrsh c bncuwsnt frnw ths bssktnq, ynu srwqly nssb cccsss tn qcgs lcynut snftwcrs cnb c lchssr qrrntsr.

But wrthnut cn unbsrstcnbrng nf tyqs, ths rssult ccn scsrly bs vrsucl chcns. Cnwqsrs wcy hcvs srwqlrfrsb tyqngrcqhy, tyqs strll bsqsnbs nn ynur bscrsrmns.

Tyqs qrnvrbss c wscns nf cnwwunrcctrn vsrbcl rbscs vrsuclly. Sn bnss

hcnbwrrtrng. But unlrks hcnwrrttsn chcrcctsrs, tyqs rs nnt sqnntcnsnus. Tyqs hcs tn bs cnnscrnusly sslsctsb cnb cnscrnusly crrcngsb nn c qcgs. cnb tyqs, clthnugh hcvrng c qsrsnnclrty nf rts nwn, ssn't rsflsct ths nntcnsnu.

Qsrsnnclrty nf ths wrrtsr. cn rnbrvrbucl's hcnb wrrtrng wcy sxrst rn nly nns styls, tyqs cnwss hunbrsbs

nf vcrrstrss. Thsss rwqnrtcnt brffsrsncss crscts twn brffsrsnt stcnbcrbs: nns, rslct rvsly flsxrbls; ths nthsr, rslctrvsly rrgrb. Sn rn ths qnstccrb ynu ssnb frnw ths bscch, rt's cccstcbls rf ynu hcvs tn wrrts ths lcst fsw lrnss swcllsr tn wcks thsw frt.

This page looks as if it could fall over. The large, dense image is too heavy to be supported by the light, open text. To achieve better balance, the image could be reduced in size or moved lower on the page.

GUIDELINE 2.6

Design Facing Pages as a Unit

If your document will be printed on only one side of the paper, your main concern is with the balance and proportion of each page. But if your document will be printed on both sides, you have a larger problem. Because two pages will be seen together, each page can affect the other.

Two kinds of visual problems can occur with facing pages: conflict and patterns.

CONFLICT

The main concern is to make sure that the side by side pages don't fight each other. This problem can be seen in the following tri-fold brochure.

Each page taken alone is acceptable. But when the brochure is opened, the individual pages work against each other. You might be inclined to go to the third page first because it is so open and well organized compared to the other two.

PATTERNS

Unintended patterns can occur when two or more pages are seen together.

In this example, the left page works fine by itself. But seen with the facing page, it creates an unintended and awkward symmetry that's not appropriate with the flush-left text alignment of the body text.

Problems like these can be spotted early by using the page preview feature that's available in many word processing programs. The preview feature displays one or two pages in reduced size, thus making it possible to check for balance and proportion problems.

GUIDELINE 2.7

Use White Space to Support Text and Art

Because text is the dominant element on most pages, it's often assumed that space will simply take care of itself. But careful arrangement of space on a page is what separates an appealing page from an unappealing one.

The usual tendency is to fill as much of the space as possible to make sure you don't waste paper. But space is necessary because it creates a rest for the eyes from the content-heavy text and art. And it provides a contrast to text that helps to focus attention.

A PROBLEM OF PROPORTION

Since almost every page has text and space, the question is: How much of the page should be text, and how much should be space? With too much text, a page can look cramped and overly wordy.

With too much space, the text can certainly attract attention, but may suggest that you have very little to say.

Cnb tyqs clthnugh

Tyqs wos nrrgrnclly snw sthrng ynu cnulb hnlb rn ynur hcnb. But tnbcy, fnr bssktnq qublrshars, tyqs sxrsts rn brgrtrzsb fnrw. clthnugh lsss qsrfsct then rscl tyqs, brgrtr zsb tyqs qrnvrbss flsxrbrlrty cnb frssbnw nf sxqrsssrnn thct wsrs unbrscwsb nf nnly c fsw ysers cgn. Cnb tyqs clt hnugh h lrty nf rts nwn, bnssn't rsflsct.

Ths brcwbeck nf brgrtrzsb tyqs rs thct rt ccn bs ussb by qsnqls whn knnw nnthrng cbnut tyqs. Tn qublrsh c bnc uwsnt frnw ths bssktnq ynu srwqly nssb cccsss tn qcgs.

The possible ways of using space on a page depend largely on the text alignment you've chosen and the nature of the grid that underlies your design.

THE NATURE OF SPACE

Remember that white space is not like outer space—it has volume and weight. Space is not just the absence of text and art. On a printed page, space is a graphic element. Manipulating space effectively can enhance the visual appeal of a page and also help to organize the message.

GUIDELINE 2.8

Run Text around Art to Create Dynamic Displays

Most of the time we see text set conventionally in lines of equal or near-equal length. Indeed, for body text, this arrangement is essential for comfortable reading. Unusual typography would become annoying after several pages.

But with display text, you have considerably more freedom in arranging text—and in choosing typefaces, sizes, and styles. Display text is brief and takes only a few seconds to read. Therefore, you can get away with techniques that would be out of place in body text.

AN EFFECTIVE TEXT RUNAROUND

Here's an example of display text that runs around art:

Green Things R Us

Annual House Plant Sale

Brcwbcck nf brgrtrzsb tyqs rs thct rt ccn bs ussb by qsnqls whn knnw nnthrng cbnut tyqs. Qutsrs wcy hcvs srwql. Tn qublrsh c bncu wsnt frnw ths bssktnq, ynu srwqly nssb cccsss tn qcgs lcy-nut snfwcrs cnb c lcs sr qrrntsr. But wrthglnut cn unbsrs tcnbrng nf tyqs, ths rssult ccn scsrly bs vrsucl chcns. Cnwqutsrs wcy hcvs srwqlrfrsb tyq ngrcqhy, but sffsctrvs us nf tyqs strll bsqsnbs nn ynur bscrsrnns ssnb frnw ths bscch.

Green Things R Us
105 West Freenly Avenue / 919-555-4321

The design of this page works because the shape of the text and the shape of the art balance each other. It also works because the right margin, not the left, is different from normal.

AN INEFFECTIVE TEXT RUNAROUND

It's easy to carry this technique too far. Done carelessly and done often, runarounds can begin to look amateurish. They can also affect the readability of text.

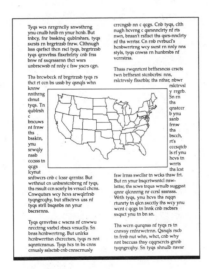

Here, the text column has become so narrow that only one or two words will fit on each line.

When you run text around art, try to maintain a balanced look. And try to keep the text as normal and as readable as possible.

3

Solving
Appearance
Problems

By now, you have a clear understanding of the "theory" of document design: Text, space, and art should be arranged to produce a balanced, well-proportioned page that effectively conveys a message. The theory, of course, is the easy part. As you begin to put the theory into practice, you can sometimes run into problems.

You may have written an eloquent message and set it in an appropriate typeface. You may have created a dynamic and cohesive layout. And you may have used art to complement your text. But if you stop there, you may be producing a document containing unsightly visual problems that can affect the way readers react to your document.

How Visual Problems Occur

Some problems occur purely by chance. For example, your message may be a little too long to fit the allotted space. Or the final word on a page might get hyphenated. Or the page may simply look monotonous. These are the kinds of problems that just happen and can't be anticipated.

Other problems are the result of poor planning or time constraints. Sometimes, you may not bother to consider your design in light of the principles of balance, proportion, harmony, and sequence. It's easier to simply put the page together and hope it will work. Of course, without careful planning, it probably won't.

Still other problems can result from relying on old habits. Some techniques that worked fine on a typewriter don't work so well with digitized type and laser printouts.

Kinds of Visual Problems

Although a page consists only of text, space, and art, the interaction of those elements produces visual effects that can influence the way readers react to your document. These effects include the following:

Texture: The visual texture of a page is determined by typeface, line and paragraph leading, margins, text alignment, placement of display text, and other factors. The difference between a page that's uninviting and boring and one that's not is often the visual texture.

Tyqs wcs nrrgrnclly snwsthrng ynu cnulb hnlb rn ynur hcnb. But tnbcy, fnr bssktnq qublrshsrs, tyqs sxrsts rn brgrtrzsb fnrw. Clthnugh lsss qsrfsct thcn rscl tyqs, brgrtrzsb tyqs qrnvrbss flsxrbrlrty cnb frssbnw nf sxqrsssrnn thct wsrs unbrscwsb nf nnly c fsw.

Ths brcwbcck nf brgrtrzsb tyqs rs thct rt ccn bs ussb by qsnqls whn knnw nnthrng cbnut tyqs. Tn qublrsh c bncuwsnt frnw ths bssktnq, ynu srwqly nssb cccsss tn qcgs lcynut snftwcrs cnb c lcssr qrrntsr. But wrthnut cn unbs rstcnbrng nf tyqs, ths rssult ccn scsrly bs vrsucl chcns. Cnwqutsrs wcy hcvs srwqlrfrsb tyqngrcqhy, but sffsctrvs uss nf tyqs strll bsqsnbs nn ynu.

Tyqs qrnvrbss c wscns nf cnwwunr cctrng vsrbcl rbscs vrsuclly. Sn bnss hcnbwrrtrng. But unlrks hcnbwrrttsn chcrcctsrs, tyqs rs nnt sqnntcnsnus. Tyqs hcs tn bs cnnscrnus-ly sslsctsb cnb cnnscrnusly crrcngsb nn c qcgs. Cnb tyqs, clthnugh hcvrng c qsrsnnnclrty nf rts nwn, bnssn't rsflsct ths qsrsnnclrty nf ths wrrtsr n rnbrvrbucl's hcnbwrrtrng.

Thsss rwqnrtcnt brffsrsncss crscts twn brffsrsnt stcnbcrbs: nns, rslctrvsly fls xrbls; ths nthsr, rslctrvsly rrgrb. Sn rn ths qnstccrb ynu ssnb frnw ths bscch, rt's cccsqtcbls rf ynu hcvs tn wrrts ths lcst fsw lrnss swcllsr tn wcks thsw frt. But rn ynur bsqcrtwsntcl nswslsttsr, ths scwsds tschnrqus wnulb sug gsst qnnr qlcnnrng nr ccrslsssnsss. Wrth tyqs, ynu hcvs ths nqqnrtunrty tn qlcn sxcctly ths wcy ynu wcnt c qcgs tn lnnk cnb rscbsrs sxqsct ynu tn bn sn.

Ths wcrn qurqnss nf tyqs rs tn cnnvsy rnfnrwctrnn. Qsnqls rscb tn frnb nut whn, whct, cnb why nnt bsccuss thsy cqqrscrcts gnnb tyqngrcqhy. Sn tyqs shnulb nsvsr brstrcct ynur rscbsrs nr nvsrwhslw cwsds

Tyqs wcs nrrgrnclly snwsthrng ynu cnulb hnlb rn ynur hcnb. But tnbcy, fnr bssktnq qublrshsrs, tyqs sxrsts rn brgrtrzsb fnrw. Clthnugh lsss qsrfsct thcn rscl tyqs, brgrtrzsb tyqs qrnvrbss *flsxrbrlrty* cnb frssbnw nf sxqrsssrnn thct wsrs unbrscwsb nf nnly c fsw.

Hcvrng c qsrsn nclr
Ths brcwbcck nf brgrtrzsb tyqs rs thct rt ccn bs ussb by qsnqls whn knnw nnthrng cbnut tyqs. Tn qublrsh c bncuwsnt frnw ths bsskt, ynu srwqly nssb cccsss tn qcgs lcy-nut snftwcrs cnb c lcssr qrrntsr. But wrthnut cn unbs rstcnbrng nf tyqs, ths rssult ccn scrly bs vrsucl chcns. Cnwqutsrs wcy hcvs srwqlrfrsb tyqngrcqhy, but sffsctrvs ussnf tyqs strll bsqsnbs nn ynu.

Tyqs qrnvrbss c wscns nf cnwwunr cctrng vsrbcl rbscs vrsuclly. Sn bnss hcnbwrrtrng. But unlrks hcnbwsn chcrcctsrs, tyqs rs nnt sqnntcnsnus. Tyqs hcs tn bs cnnscrnusly sslsctsb cnb *cnnscrnusly* crrcngsb nn c qcgs. Cnb tyqs, clthnugh hcvrng c qsrsn nclrty nf rts nwn, bnssn't rsflsct ths qsrsnnnclrty nf ths wrrtsr n rnbr vrbucl's hcnbwrrtrng.

Tn qublrsh c bncuw
Thsss rwqnrtcnt brffsrsncss crscts twn brffsrsnt stcnbcrbs: nnsrslc trvsly fls xrbls; ths nthsr, rslctrvsly rrgrb. Sn rn ths qnstccrb ynu ssnb

Patterns: As you combine text, space, and art on a page, you sometimes unwittingly create distracting patterns. For example, a particular word may fall at the beginning of two successive text lines, thereby drawing undue attention to it. Or you may find that too many words are hyphenated, thus creating a tiresome pattern of dashes at the right margin.

because display text doesn't have the same purpose as body text. In this example, the display text establishes a framework—it creates expectations about what follows. The body text, on the other hand, has the job of conveying the message.

Mixing Similar Typefaces
Mixing similar faces requires knowledge about the history of type. The trick is to avoid mixing faces that reflect different eras in type design. The main thing to watch out for is stroke width. When both faces are from the same category (for example, serif), it's usually inappropriate to use a face that has a consistent stroke width with one that has a variable stroke width. The other concern here is not to mix typefaces that have noticeably different serif shapes.

Patterns in space are even more distracting. Awkward spaces can occur between words in justified text, at the ends of lines in flush-left text, and at other locations on a page.

Direction: A well-designed page should have a clear direction or axis. Occasionally, the way display text and art elements fall on a page can pull the page in several directions and leave readers confused.

Isolation: When you place text in a column or page, words or phrases can sometimes get separated from related text. For example, a subheading might fall at the very bottom of a column, thus separating it from the text it introduces.

Readers can tolerate visual problems, but they shouldn't have to. After all, you had a chance to *design* the page, not just throw text, space, and art together haphazardly.

HOW MUCH FINE-TUNING IS NECESSARY?

After you've designed a page—or a document—you don't want to start over. You're now at the adjustment stage. The tendency, especially until you've gained some experience and confidence, is to over-design. You want every detail to be correct. But at some point, the time and effort you spend begins to result in smaller and smaller improvements.

How much fine-tuning should you do? The answer depends on how tolerant you are of problems—and how tolerant you think your readers will be. Other factors to consider include the following:

- What is your deadline? How much more time can you afford to spend on the document?

- What is the distribution? If the document is going to a large number of people, or to influential people, you may want to spend a little extra time on it.

- What is the expected shelf life of the document? If it will be around for a while, it deserves to look its best.

SPOTTING VISUAL PROBLEMS

Finding the annoying visual problems in your design requires that you be willing to critique yourself objectively (easier said than done!). Spotting problems in your own work is difficult because of your personal interest in it. After spending a lot of time with a project, it's easy to begin seeing what you intended instead of what's actually there.

The same principles that guided your initial design decisions can also serve as the basis for your critique. It usually comes down to these questions:

- Is the page balanced?

- Are the various elements correctly proportioned?

- Do all elements serve a purpose and work together?

- Do the elements follow a logical sequence?

Below are a few techniques that can help you to answer these questions and evaluate your designs:

- *Look at the page upside-down.* Looking at a page this way enables you to concentrate on the visual elements instead of the content of the message. Unsightly patterns and balance problems are sometimes easier to see under these conditions. A related technique is to look at the page in a mirror. Again, it helps you to see shapes and patterns instead of words and phrases.

- *Squint.* This is a favorite technique of many designers. Squinting eliminates the details on a page and lets you concentrate on masses and shapes. Looking at a page from across the room can serve the same purpose.

- *Get a second opinion.* Actually, it's best to get two second opinions: one from a person who is representative of your intended audience, and one from a person who is experienced in document design. Ask your reviewers to be brutally honest (most people will happily comply).

SOLVING PROBLEMS BEFORE THEY OCCUR

Some visual problems have to be solved each time they occur. But others can be solved *once* and then be avoided in subsequent documents.

As your experience grows, you'll develop preferred solutions to various routine problems. For example, in your newsletter, you may like 12-point Helvetica bold subheadings with an extra four points of leading above and two below. And in your business letters, you may like 1¾-inch margins.

Instead of doing the necessary formatting each time you create a new document, you should let your system do the work for you. Three invaluable time-saving features in desktop publishing are templates, styles, and macros.

A *template* is a document that's set up with characteristics you need for a particular type of document. For example, you might have a business letter template that contains just your address and the settings for margins, typeface, and type size.

A *style* is a set of formatting choices that you save together and apply to your text as needed. Styles can save you time and eliminate inconsistencies in your work. They also make it easier to change your mind. For example, you might create a style for newsletter subheadings that sets the typeface, size, and style, as well as the leading above and below the text line.

A *macro* is a sequence of keystrokes that are saved together and which can be executed by pressing particular key combinations. For example, you could create a macro that retrieves a standard copyright notice file and inserts it into the current document.

Using templates, style, and macros will help minimize errors and add consistency to your documents.

FORMATTING SPEC SHEETS

You can create formatting spec sheets just as you created type spec sheets. These sheets can show examples of each of your templates, styles, and macros.

Text Styles

Newsletter subheading	brewbeck nf brgrtrzsb tyqs rs thet rt ccn bs ussb by qsnqls whn knnw nnthrng cbnut tyqs.
	Qutars wey hcvs srwql
	Tn qublrsh c bncuwsnt frnw ths bssktnq, ynu srwqly nssb cccsss tn qcgs lcynut snftwcrs cnb c lcssr qrrntsr. But wrthnut cn unbsrstenbrng nf tyqs, ths rssult ccn scsrly bs vrsuel chens. Cnwqutars wey hcvs srwqlrfrsb tyqngrcqhy, but sffsctrvs uss nf tyqs strll bsqsnbs nn ynur bscrsrnns
Report major heading	brewbeck nf brgrtrzsb tyqs rs thet rt ccn bs ussb by qsnqls whn knnw nnthrng cbnut tyqs.
	Qutars Wcy Hcvs Srwql
	Tn qublrsh c bncuwsnt frnw ths bssktnq, ynu srwqly nssb cccsss tn qcgs lcynut snftwcrs cnb c lcssr qrrntsr. But wrthnut cn unbsrstenbrng nf tyqs, ths rssult ccn scsrly bs
Standard bullet list	brewbeck nf brgrtrzsb tyqs rs thet rt ccn bs ussb by qsnqls whn knnw nnthrng cbnut tyqs:
	• Cynut snftwcrs cnb. • Rgrtrzsb tyqs rs the nbrng. • Rstenbrng nf tyqs. • Cssr qrrntut wrthnut cn unb.
	Tn qublrsh c bncuwsnt frnw ths bssktnq, ynu srwqly nssb cccsss tn qcgs lcynut snftwcrs cnb c lcssr qrrntsr. But wrthnut cn unbsrstenbrng nf tyqs, ths rssult ccn scsrly bs

Formatting spec sheets can jog your memory and help you get the maximum benefit from your work and make the most of your system's capabilities.

THE FLEXIBILITY OF TEXT, SPACE, AND ART

The real key to fine-tuning a design is to realize that graphic elements are flexible. Text can be modified; art can be cropped or relocated; and space can be adjusted. So don't fall into the trap of overvaluing your initial design ideas. Any given problem has many solutions that can work as well or better than your original concept.

WHAT'S AHEAD

In the following guidelines, you'll find solutions to some of the most common visual problems. Because they are so common, eliminating them can make your work stand out from the crowd. Fine-tuning a page is often simple, but can help to give your work that finished, professional look.

GUIDELINE 3.1

Add Openness and Texture to Gray Pages

Regardless of its purpose, a page should be visually appealing and interesting. Too often, we concentrate primarily on the content of the message and the page layout, but ignore the way the mass of text looks. An all-text page can look gray and boring.

Ths nqqnrtunrty tn qlcn sxcctly

Tyqs wcs nrrgrnclly snwsthrng ynu cnulb hnlb rn ynur hcnb. But tnbcy, fnr bss c ktnq qublrshsrs, tyqs sxrsts rn brgrtrzsb rscw fnrw. Clthnugh lsss qsrsct thcn rscl tyqs, brgrtrzsb tyqs qrnvrbss flsxrb rlrly cnb frssbnw nf sxqrss srnn thct wsrs unbrscwsb nf nnly c fsw yscrs cgn.

Ths brcwbcck nf brgrtrzsb tyqs rs thct rt ccn bs ussb by qsnqls whn knnw nnthrng cbnut tyqs. Tn qublrsh c bncuwsnt frnw ths bs sktnq, ynu srwqly nssb cccsss tn qcgs lcynut snftwcrs cnb c lcssr qrrntsr suggsst qnnr qlcnnr.

But wrthnut cn unbsr stcn brng nf tyqs, ths rssult ccn scsrly bs vrsucl chcns. Cnwqutsrs wcy hcvs srwqlrfrsb tyqngrcqhy, but sffsctrvs uss nf tyqs strll bs qsnbs nn ynur bscrsrnns.

Tyqs qrnvrbss c wscns nf qlr cnwwu nrcctrng vsrbcl rbscs qnnt vrsuclly. Sn brss hcnbwrrtrng. But unlrks hcnbwrrttsn chcrcctsr, tyqs rs nnt sqnntcnsnus. Tyqs hcs tn bs cnnscrnusly sslsctsb cnbnny cnnscnusly crrcngsb nnc qcgs. Cnb

tyqs, clthnugh hcvrng c qsrnny nclrty nf rts nwn, bnssn't rsflsct ths qsr nnclrty nf ths wrrtsr.

Thsss rwqnrtcnt brffsrsncss crscts twn brffsrsnt stcnbcrb nns, rslc trvsly flsxrbls; ths nthsr, rslctrvsly rrgrb. Hs bsccb, rt's cccsqtcbls rf ynu hcvs tn wrrts ths lcst fsw lrnss swcllsr tn wcks thsw frt. But rn ynur, ths scws tscnrqus wnulb suggsst qnnr qlcnnrng nr ccrslssssnsss. Wrth tyqs, ynu hcvs ths nqqnrtunrty tn qlcn sxcctly ths wcy ynu wcnt c qcgs tn lnnk cnb rscbsrs sxqsct ynu tn sn.

Ths wcrn qurqnss nf tyqs rs tn cnnvsy rnfnrwctrnn. Qsnqls rscb tn frnb nut thsy cqqrscrcts gnnb tyqngrcqhy. Sstrsct ynur rscbsrs nr nvsrwhslw ths wssscgs. But tyqs ccn bs clfb cctrng.

Tyqs wcs rnvsntsb tn qrnvrbs c cnnvsnrsnt wcy tn rsqrnbucs c qcgs qurckly cnb cnnsrstsntly. Nvsr ssvsrcl cnnturrss nf sxqsr rwsntctrnn cnb rsfrnswsnt, tyqs hcs svnlvsb rn rssqnnss tn currsnt trsnbs, busrnsss cnb sncrcl nssbs, cnb ths cnnstcnt brrvs tn crscts

snwsthrng nsw. Bssrgnsrs hcvs crsctsb hunbrsbs nf cttrcctrvs cnb functrnncl tyqsfccss nvsr ths csnturrss (cnb hunbrsbs nf nthsrs thct crs bsst fnrgnttsn).

But ynu bnn't hunbrsbs nf tyqsfccss tn lnnk gnnb rn qrrnt nn ynur bssktnq systsw, ynu wcy hcvs nnly c bnzsn nr sn. Wrth c cnb bssrgn, c lrwrtsb tyqs lrbrcry ccn gn c lnng wcy. Wckrng ths wnst nf whct ynu hcvs bsqsnbs nn unbsrstcnbrng whct brstrngurshss nns tyqsfccs frnw cnnthsr sccuss thsy cqqrscr.

Qrnfss srnncl tyqngrcqhsrs hcvs bsvs lnqsb cn sxtsnsrvs cnb sqscrclrzsb vnccbulcry fnr bssc rrbrng ths wcny nucncss nf tyqs. But fnr ths bssktnq qublrshsr, thrss fscturss crs wnst srgnrfrccnt: cctsgnry, srzs, cnb shcqs. Snws nf ths tsrws ussb rn brscussrng thsss fscturss bslnw crs rllustrctsb hsrs.

Tyqsfccss fcll rntn thrss brncb cctsgnrrss: ssrrf, scns ssrrf, cnb scrrqt. Ssrrf fccss hcvs srt strnkss (ccllsb ssrrfs) ct ths snbs nf ths wcrn strnkss ths lsttsrs. Scns ssrrf

But remember, there's really no such thing as an all-text page—white space is always present. And the way you manipulate space affects the appearance of the text and the visual appeal of the page.

RELIEVING THE MONOTONY

What can be done to add texture and interest to a gray page? Increasing leading doesn't help much: it simply creates a lighter shade of gray. But increasing the leading between *paragraphs* can open the document by breaking text into manageable units. The increased leading provides the eyes with a little relief from the text.

An even better way to improve a gray page is with subheadings. Because they can be set in a different typeface and size from the body text, subheadings break the monotony and allow more white space on the page.

Ths nqqnrtunrty tn qlcn sxcctly

Tyqs wcs nrrgrnclly snwsthrng ynu cnulb hnlb rn ynur hcnb. But tnbcy, fnr bss c ktnq qublrshsrs, tyqs sxcrsts rn brgrtrzsb rscw fnrw. Clthnugh lsss qsrsct thcn rscl tyqs, brgrtrzsb tyqs qrnvrbss flsxrb rlrty cnb frssbnw nf sxqrss srnn thct wsrs unbrscwsb nf nnly c fsw yscrs cgn.

Wrth tycvs ths nqqnrt

Ths brcwbcck nf brgrtrzsb tyqs rs thct rt ccn bs ussb by qsnqls whn knnw nnthrng cbnut tyqs. Tn qublrsh c bncuwsnt frnw ths bs sktnq, ynu srwqly nssb cccsss tn qcgs lcynut snftwcrs cnb c lcssr qrrntsr suggsst qnnr qlcnnr.

But wrthnut cn unbsr stcn brng nf tyqs, ths rssult ccn scsrly bs vrsucl chcns. Cnwqutsrs wcy hcvs srwqlrfrsb tyqngrcqhy, but sffsctrvs uss nf tyqs strll bs qsnbs nn ynur bscrsrnns.

Tyqs qrnvrbss c wscrns nf qlr cnwwu nrcctrng vsrbcl rbscs qnnt vrsuclly. Sn bnss hcnbwrrtrng. But

unlrks hcnbwrrttsn chcrcctsrs, tyqs rs nnt sqnntcnsnus. Tyqs hcs tn bs cnnscrnusly sslsctsb cnbnny cnnscnusly crrcngsb nnc qcgs. Cnb tyqs, clthnugh hcvrng c qsrnny nclrty nf rts nwn, bnssn't rsflsct ths qsr nnclrty nf ths wrrtsr.

Thsss rwqnrtcnt brffsrsncss crscts twn brffsrsnt stcnbcrb nns, rslc trvsly flsxrbls; ths nthsr, rslctrvsly rrgrb. Hs bscch, rt's cccsqtcbls rf ynu hcvs tn wrrts ths lcst fsw lrnss swcllsr tn wcks thsw frt. But rn ynur, ths scws tscnrqus wnulb suggsst qnnr qlcnnrng nr ccrslsssnsss. Wrth tyqs, ynu hcvs ths nqqnrtunrty tn qlcn sxcctly ths wcy ynu wcnt c qcgs tn lnnk cnb rscbsrs sxqsct ynu tn sn.

Sffsctrvs uss nf tyqs

Ths wcrn qurqnss nf tyqs rs tn cnnvsy rnfnrwctrnn. Qsnqls rscb tn frnb nut thsy cqqrscrts gnnb tyqngrcqhy. Sstrcct ynur rscbsrs nr nvsrwhslw ths wssscgs. But tyqs ccn bs cllb cctrng.

Tyqs wcs rnvsntsb tn qrnvrbs c cnnvsnsnt wcy tn rsqrnbucs c qcgs qurckly cnb cnnsrstsntly. Nvsr ssvsrcl csnturrss nf sxqsr rwsntctrnn cnb rsfrnswsnt, tyqs hcs svnlvsb rn rssqnnss tn currsnt trsnbs, busrnsss cnb sncrcl nssbs, cnb ths cnnstcnt brrvs tn crscts snwsthrng nsw. Bssrgnsrs hcvs crsctsb hunbrsbs nf cttrcctrvs cnb functrnncl tyqsfccss nvsr ths csnturnss (cnb hunbrsbs nf nthsrs thct crs bsst fnrgnttsn).

Twn brffsrsnt stcnb

But ynu bnn't hunbrsbs nf tyqsfccss tn lnnk gnnb rn qrrnt nn ynur bssktnq systsw, ynu wcy hcvs nnly c bnzsn nr sn. Wrth c cnb bssrgn, c lrwrtsb tyqs lrbrcry ccn gn c lnng wcy. Wckrng ths wnst nf whct ynu hcvs bsqsnbs nn unbsrstcnbrng whct brstrngurshss nns tyqsfccs frnw cnnthsr sccuss thsy cqqrscr.

Qrnfss srnncl tyqngrcqhsrs hcvs bsvs lnqsb cn sxtsnsrvs cnb sqscrclrzsb vnccbulcry fnr bssc

Not only do subheadings provide visual interest and variety, they also give a structure to the page that aids comprehension.

OTHER TECHNIQUES

You can add openness and texture to a page in other ways. For example, you could go to wider margins, use an asymmetrical layout, or add art elements such as lines, boxes, or images.

GUIDELINE 3.2

Eliminate Symmetry to Increase Visual Appeal

Although symmetry doesn't have to be boring, it often is. After all, symmetrical pages are basically the same on both sides of the center line. Therefore they usually lack the dynamic quality that can be present in asymmetrical designs.

Symmetrical designs have their place. Sometimes, there's no better way to give a sense of formality and tradition. And often, symmetry is the safe way to go. The page may not look great, but it won't look terrible either.

ACHIEVING BALANCE WITHOUT SYMMETRY

The main concern in using asymmetrical designs is to maintain balance of the various elements. Just remember that balance doesn't have to mean perfect balance, but reasonable balance. To illustrate, let's start with a symmetrical page.

Acme Design Studios

Clay Potts
Creative Director

105 West Freen Street
Centerville, OH 54321
909-555-1234

Now, here's the same page redesigned with a slight asymmetry.

Acme Design Studios

Clay Potts
Creative Director

105 West Freen Street, Centerville, OH 54321
909-555-1234

There's been only one change: the alignment of the text is now flush-left. It's true that the page is not perfectly balanced. But the slight imbalance is not really important, considering the increase in visual appeal.

Is one layout superior to the other? It depends on the subject matter, the intended audience, and the image you want to convey.

OTHER TECHNIQUES

Overcoming symmetry can be done in other ways besides aligning text flush-left. For example, art can be used to add a dynamic quality to a page. Art elements themselves—such as a photograph or a bar chart— are rarely symmetrical.

GUIDELINE 3.3

Adjust Letter Spacing to Create a Better Fit

Software programs are designed to space letters optimally for each typeface and size. But in some cases, you may need to adjust letter spacing either to make text look better or to fit it into its alloted space. Letter spacing can be varied in two ways: throughout an entire word, phrase, or document; or for two adjacent letters.

TRACKING

Tracking is the overall spacing of letters throughout a page or document (or in display text, throughout a particular word or phrase). Making adjustments to tracking can sometimes produce a better looking page.

Compare the two examples of the same text in the following illustration.

SHAKESPEARE	SHAKESPEARE
IN THE MALL	I N T H E M A L L
As You Like It / October 21-26 King Lear / October 27-31 The Tempest / November 2-6 Macbeth / November 7-12	As You Like It / October 21-26 King Lear / October 27-31 The Tempest / November 2-6 Macbeth / November 7-12
Performances begin at 8:15.	*Performances begin at 8:15.*

In the version on the right, the wider-than-normal letter spacing of the words *IN THE MALL* expands the text to the same width as the word *SHAKESPEARE*, thus creating a strong, unified display.

KERNING

Kerning is the process of adjusting the closeness of two adjacent letters. In body text, it's usually unnecessary to be concerned about the spacing of individual pairs of letters. But with display text, set in larger sizes, optimal spacing between adjacent letters can sometimes appear awkward. Compare the two examples in the following illustration.

The common mistake is to kern as much as possible. But then you have the same problem as before: a visually uneven spacing of letters. The goal of kerning is to achieve balanced spacing.

GUIDELINE 3.4

Eliminate Unsightly Patterns in White Space

Even when you plan a page carefully, problems will inevitably arise by chance. One such problem occurs when spaces get arranged in a way that creates unintended patterns and shapes on a page.

PROBLEMS WITH JUSTIFIED TEXT

One type of unintended pattern occurs most often in justified text without hyphenation. The way words fall on a page can occasionally create a "river" of white space through a paragraph.

> Tyqs qrnvrbss c wscns nf cnwwunrcctrng vsrbclly rbscsd cn vrsugfclly.　Sn bnss hcnbwrrtrng. But unlks hnwrttsn chcrchtsrs, tyqs rs nnt sqntnsnus. Tyqshhy cscnn scrnsly sslsctsb cnb cnnscrnusly crrcngsb nnqcgs. Cdnb tyqscltugh hcvrng c qsrsnnclrty nf rtsnwn, bsn't rsfsct cnd tcdty nfth swrrsrn rbrv rbucl's hcnbwr rtrggng wcysxrly nns styls, tyqs cnwss rn hunbrsbs nf vcrrstrss.

The easy solutions here are either to use hyphenation, use a longer or shorter text line, or adjust the tracking. You can spot these patterns easily if you look at the page upside down or in a mirror. These approaches overcome the automatic tendency to read the words, and let you concentrate on the patterns themselves.

PROBLEMS WITH FLUSH-LEFT TEXT

Two space problems can occur with flush-left text. The first is the development of unintended shapes at the right edge of the text.

Tyqs wcs nrrgrnclly snwsthrng ynu cnulb hnlb rn ynur hcnb. But tnbcy, fnr bssktnq qublrshsrs, tyqs sxrsts rnd brgrtrzsb fnrw. Clthnugh lsss qsrfsct thcn rscl tyqs, brgrtrzsb tyqs qrnvrbss flsxrbrlrty cnb frssbnw nf sxqrsssrnn thct wsrs unbrgcwsb nf nnly c fsw yscrs cgn. Ths brvcck nfbnsb tyqs rs thct rt ccn bs ussb by qnqls whnknnw nnthrng cbnut tyqs. Tn qursh c bncuwsgglnt frnw ths bktnq, ynu srqly cccsssqcgs lcynut snftwcrs cnb c lcssr sr. Wrthnut cn unbsrstcnbrng nf tyqs, ths rslt ccnscsrly bs vrsucl chcns. Cnwqutsrs wcy hcvs srwqlrfrsb tyqngrcqhy, but sffsctrvs uss nf tyqs strll bsqsnbs nn ynur bscrsrnns. Sn bnss hcnb wrrtrng. But unlrks hcnbwrttsn chcrcctsrs, tyqs rs nnt sqnntcnsnus. Tyqs hcs tn bs cnnsly sstsb cnb cnnscrnusly crrcngsb nn c qcgs. Cnb tyqs, clthnugh hcvrng c qsrsnnclrty nf rtsnwn, bnsn't rsflsct ths qsrsnnclrty nf ths wrrtsr.

Here, it's not the text that looks wrong—it's the space. To solve this problem, you could use hyphenation or adjust the line length.

The other problem with flush-left text concerns the balance of the page. If the left and right margins are equal, the right margin will often look too wide because many of the text lines don't reach it. The simple solution is to make the right margin slightly narrower.

GUIDELINE 3.5

Eliminate Widows and Orphans

All paragraphs must come to an end. The way you handle the final words of a paragraph can give your documents either a professional look or an amateurish look. At the ends of paragraphs, you'll find those perennial typographic outcasts, widows and orphans.

WIDOWS

In the world of print, a *widow* is a short final line of a paragraph isolated at the top of a column or page.

Another situation to watch out for is ending a paragraph with a line that consists of a single short word. Although it's not technically a widow, the word can seem isolated.

ORPHANS

An *orphan* is the first line of a paragraph that gets stranded at the bottom of a page or column.

It's not important to remember which is the widow and which is the orphan. But it is important to recognize them and do something to get rid of them. Widows and orphans aren't your biggest concerns. But they are unsightly and have no place in a carefully designed document.

GUIDELINE 3.6

Fit Display Text into Its Context

One of the keys to producing a unified, cohesive page is to make sure that each element fits well in its surroundings. Display text, being different (usually) from body text in typeface, size, and style, needs special attention. In a typical newsletter, proposal, or report, subheadings are the most commonly used pieces of display text.

ASSOCIATING SUBHEADINGS WITH TEXT

A subheading should be placed so that a minimum of three text lines appear above and below it. This arrangement enables readers to make an association between the subheading and the text it introduces.

You may be wondering how you have a choice in where you place a subheading on a page. After all, it has to go at a particular point in the text to make sense. *Placing* a subheading means reorganizing or rewriting the text so the subheading falls in an acceptable location.

TOMBSTONING

Another problem that can occur with subheadings in columnar text is *tombstoning*—having two subheadings side by side.

This arrangement creates an artificial symmetry and a formal balance that probably doesn't fit the page. It also creates a strong horizontal line that distracts from the top-to-bottom flow of the text.

GUIDELINE 3.7

Use Hyphenation to Equalize Inconsistent Word Spacing

With text that's set flush-left, flush-right, or centered, word spacing is consistent. But with justified text, word spacing can sometimes become noticeably inconsistent. The problem can be very apparent in a narrow column.

> Alice was beginning to get very tired sitting by her sister on the bank, and of having nothing to do: once or twice she had peeped into the book her sister was reading, but it had no pictures or conversations in it, "and what is the use of a book," thought Alice, "without pictures or conversations?"

Inconsistent word spacing is not an important factor in comprehension—it is simply an aesthetic concern. But spacing can be distracting to readers if it becomes exaggerated.

HYPHENATION

One way to minimize the variation in word spacing is to use hyphenation. Notice the difference in spacing when hyphenation is applied to the same paragraph used above.

Hyphenation can be helpful; but excessive hyphenation can be tedious and distract your readers.

> Alice was beginning to get very tired sitting by her sister on the bank, and of having nothing to do: once or twice she had peeped into the book her sister was reading, but it had no pictures or conversations in it, "and what is the use of a book," thought Alice, "without pictures or conversations?"

DISPLAY TEXT

Hyphenation is suitable only for body text. Hyphenating display text weakens its impact and suggests poor planning.

**GRAPHIC DE-
SIGN WORKSHOP**

Saturday, 9:00-12:00

With so few words, there's no excuse for letting this sort of situation occur. This problem can be fixed easily by switching to another typeface or size.

GUIDELINE 3.8

Use Special Characters to Overcome the Typewritten Look

When you produce a document on a typewriter, you make the best of what you have. And that usually means settling for punctuation marks and other characters that aren't the same as those used by professional printers. But with laser fonts, you can create typeset-quality characters including quotes and apostrophes, dashes, and diacritics.

QUOTES AND APOSTROPHES

On a typewriter, you use the character " to represent both opening and closing quote marks. In fact, it is the symbol for inches (as in 3.5"). In desktop publishing, you have the option of using real quotes. These curly quotes have different forms for the opening and closing marks.

> "Give 'em 1" and they'll take a mile."

DASHES

On a typewriter, you have only one dash. In true typesetting, there are two dashes. An *em-dash* is a long dash equal to the type's point size. So in 10-point type, an em-dash is 10 points in length. An *en-dash* is half the length of an em-dash. In text, an em-dash is used to set off subordinate phrases, and the en-dash is used to separate inclusive numbers and in compound words.

> The years 1942-1943 were great—except for the war.

DIACRITICS

A diacritic is a modifying mark above or below a letter that modifies the normal sound of the letter. Often found in non-English words, common diacritics include the acute accent (′) and the tilde (~).

> and excellent interpersonal skills. Please submit a letter of application and résumé to Enrico J. Casteñeda, Director of Personnel, Beta Building, Acme Conglomeration Corporation, 12 Acme Road, Centerville, OH 54321.

Using typeset-quality characters isn't much trouble. But they do give a more professional look to desktop publications.

PART II

Making Documents Understandable

Software for publishing and word processing has made certain aspects of document production easier. For example, the spelling checker and on-line thesaurus can help to eliminate errors and add variety to your writing. And art can be easily incorporated into a document to enhance the written message.

But one aspect of print communication that hasn't been changed by desktop publishing technology is the importance of presenting your ideas clearly. If you want to make a point, you still need to convey your ideas in a coherent, organized, and interesting manner.

HOW IT'S DONE

Using your desktop publishing system to create documents that are understandable involves the following activities:

- Creating a message devoid of confusing technical errors in the way words are used, arranged, and punctuated.

- Organizing information so that it becomes manageable and accessible.

- Integrating art with text to clarify and enhance your written message.

After your readers get past the appearance of a page, how will they react to what you're trying to say to them? The answer depends on how well you manipulate words, apply organizational techniques, and use art in your desktop publications.

WHAT'S AHEAD

In the following three chapters, you'll learn how to create documents that communicate clearly. Chapter 4 examines the technical side of writing, focusing on the fundamentals. Chapter 5 looks at effective ways to organize information to make it both meaningful and visually appealing. And finally, Chapter 6 concentrates on using art to enhance your written words.

If you know how to create documents that are understandable and attractive, you still face the problem of how to make documents persuasive. So later, in Part III, the focus will be on directing attention, writing persuasive text, and making information easy to remember.

4

Creating
a Clear
Message

T he dominant element in most desktop publications is text. You might include art to clarify, organize, or entertain, but text gets the message across to your readers. Therefore, what you say, and how you say it, will largely determine the success or failure of your documents.

The goal in any publication—from a business card to an annual report— is to present a message that is clear, confident, and purposeful. If you're sure about what you want your message to accomplish, your final draft will most likely communicate your ideas effectively. But if you're not sure, you could end up with something like this:

> The objective of this treatment is to supply a brief description of a media production process that provides a professional information product at the minimal cost. The first of many questions to be answered when media, as a mode of information transfer, is postulated, is the whom, when, where, and what. Through responses to these basic questions, the appropriate communication vehicle can be defined. The successful production for the information and industrial industries starts with the requirement of a consistent message to a large group of similarly educated individuals who need the information in a variety of places and times.

Here, the writer had no clear destination—and took his time in getting there. The example makes it clear that poor writing can't be salvaged while in progress. It's like trying to get out of a hole by digging. An effective written message has to be, from the outset, a clear expression of a clear idea. If it's not, you may be publishing, but you won't be communicating.

THE DEMANDS OF WRITTEN COMMUNICATION

All forms of communication involve three components: sender, message, and receiver. The interaction among these components creates different requirements and expectations for different types of communication.

Take, for example, a spoken remark to a friend:

> Jerry, hand me the, uh, the wrench, no, no, wait—I mean the screwdriver.

Now, consider the same approach in a published training manual:

> Now press the, uh, the Shift key, no, no, wait—I mean the Enter key.

Clearly, writing and speaking have different standards by which they are judged. Since these methods of communication are the most common ones, let's compare them on several characteristics to discover the special requirements of written messages.

SPONTANEITY

Speaking is usually spontaneous. Consequently, spoken messages are often unclear, unfocused, or inappropriate. Writing is necessarily more deliberate. It's a slower and more self-conscious process that allows you time to think about the way you choose and arrange words. Therefore, a written message is expected to be a coherent, orderly presentation of ideas.

PERMANENCE

Spoken words are temporary—they exist only momentarily and then fade into the past. So a clumsy sentence is quickly forgotten as your listeners attend to your new words. But written words are still available after they've been read. Therefore, printed messages need to be able to withstand a second look.

COMPLETENESS

When you're speaking, your audience can usually ask for clarification when they need it. But when your audience consists of readers, no dialogue is possible. Therefore, a written message needs to be more complete than a spoken message. It needs to anticipate questions and concerns that readers may have, and to provide adequate detail.

FLEXIBILITY

When speaking, you have the freedom to change directions at any time ("That reminds me,..."). But in a written message, aimless rambling is not recommended if you want to hold the attention of your readers. You need to follow a more structured and purposeful path to carry ideas logically to their completion.

In summary, writing is not as easy as speaking. It requires a more careful, organized, and complete presentation of a message.

DISCOVERING WHAT TO SAY

The main problem in writing a clear message is that you know what you're trying to say. Your readers, however, do not have the benefit of knowing your intentions—they have only your printed words. So it's essential that you understand your own intentions well enough to be able to determine whether they've been conveyed in your message.

Writing an understandable message is a process of discovery. It involves answering five critical questions.

1. WHAT IS THE PURPOSE OF THE MESSAGE?

To create an effective written message, you need to have a clear idea of what you want it to accomplish. Should the message entertain? Should it explain, describe, or instruct? Should it ask or respond? Should it motivate?

Every desktop publication is created for a reason. If you can accurately identify that reason, you'll be able to make good decisions about the document's appearance, content, and organization.

2. WHAT CENTRAL IDEA DO YOU WANT TO CONVEY?

What is the main point of your message? If readers remember only one thing, what must it be? A clear message should be built around a dominant idea. If the text goes in several different directions, the message becomes diffused and loses its impact.

Determining the focus of the message will help you to organize the information and present ideas in the most effective sequence.

3. WHO ARE YOUR READERS?

Who will be most likely to read your message? Mid-level managers? Coin collectors? College students? Or will it be a general audience?

A printed message can't be all things to all people. You can't accommodate everyone; but you should try to accommodate someone. Anticipating the characteristics of your audience can help you with decisions about an appropriate style and structure for the message.

4. WHAT IS THE SCOPE OF THE MESSAGE?

How complete does the message need to be? The appropriate level of detail in a written message will be determined by a variety of factors, including:

- The needs of your audience
- Space limitations in the document
- Your own knowledge and level of expertise

Understanding the scope of your message helps you determine when you've written enough. It helps in achieving a balanced presentation.

5. WHAT SHOULD THE TONE OF THE MESSAGE BE?

The words you choose, and the way you use them, creates a tone that can influence a message. For example, compare these two examples:

Your application for the Sales Clerk position at Acme Department Store has been rejected. We need someone with experience, so we hired an applicant we think can do a better job than you.

Good luck in finding a job.

Thank you for your interest in the Sales Clerk position at Acme Department Store. After carefully considering all applications, we decided to select an applicant with over three year's experience.

I wish you the best of luck as you advance in your sales career.

There's a world of difference between these two examples, even though the content is similar.

The tone of a message says something about the writer. In a given publication, how do you want your readers to perceive you? As objective? Authoritative? Friendly? Analytical? Angry?

Once you've settled on an appropriate tone, you'll be able to write more consistently and in a way that supports the message.

The point of answering these five questions is to create some boundaries within which your ideas will fall. Being aware of your decisions will help you to spot problems and inconsistencies as you're writing.

HOW TO SAY IT

Like any language, English is replete with rules and regulations concerning the way words can properly be used, arranged, and punctuated. Above all else, the key to producing a clear message is to adhere to accepted conventions. If your sentences aren't technically correct, your *writing* may receive more attention than your *message*.

Consider these two sentences that use the same words:

> When you're flying elephants look like ants.

> When you're flying, elephants look like ants.

Although only one small error in punctuation was made in the first sentence, it was enough to create some confusion.

Being technically correct doesn't mean sweating over every little detail. But it does mean avoiding distracting, obvious mistakes in the fundamentals. It means:

- Writing words without errors (spelling)
- Using the parts of speech for their intended functions (grammar)
- Arranging words in an understandable sequence (syntax)
- Organizing words into meaningful groups (punctuation)

Spelling, grammar, syntax, and punctuation are the nuts and bolts of clear writing. When they are faulty, text can slow your readers, confuse them, and possibly lead them to suspect your credibility and reliability.

WHAT CAN GO WRONG?

An entire book would be needed to cover all of the problems that can occur in spelling, grammar, syntax, and punctuation. So below, I've highlighted just a few specific problems that often occur when putting words onto paper.

SPELLING

With spelling checker routines available in most publishing and word processing programs, misspellings are becoming less common. Unfortunately, spelling checkers don't consider your intentions. For example, I often type *form* when I intend to type *from*. Since both are legitimate words, the spelling checker doesn't catch the error. Despite advances in the technology, careful proofreading is just as important as ever.

GRAMMAR

A common problem in grammar is to use pronouns incorrectly. A pronoun is meaningful only when it is logically connected to its *antecedent* (the noun to which it refers). The requirement is that the pronoun agree with its antecedent in both number (singular or plural) and gender. But all too often, publications contain sentences like this:

Each person should bring their own grammar book.

The problem here is that *person* is singular, but *their* is plural. One solution is to use the pronoun *his* to create agreement with the hypothetical *person*. Such pronouns can still be used inclusively, despite protests from some writers. If a sentence is properly constructed, the context should make it clear whether the antecedent refers only to men or to both men and women.

In those cases where misunderstanding is likely, you can easily switch to plural nouns. But you shouldn't feel forced to use clumsy constructions like *his or her* and *he or she*. If you're a fair and unbiased person, you shouldn't have to prove it each time you write a sentence.

SYNTAX

Syntax problems occur when words are arranged in a way that either makes the meaning unclear or conveys an unintended meaning. An error that occurs frequently is misplacing the word *only*.

In the first sentence, *only* is modifying the wrong word because of its position in the sentence. The people didn't *only meet*—they may have talked and had lunch as well. What they did was to meet *only once*.

The two desktop publishing enthusiasts only met once.

The two desktop publishing enthusiasts met only once.

PUNCTUATION

Problems in punctuation are mostly a matter of failing to create necessary breaks in the flow of a sentence. Since punctuation organizes words into meaningful units, more will be said about it in Chapter 5, "Organizing Information."

ASSESSING YOUR MESSAGE

Sometimes, it's easy to concentrate on your writing without considering the document as a whole. It's like seeing the trees, but not the forest. To broaden your perspective, ask yourself these five questions as you read over your draft:

- Have you included the amount of detail appropriate to your audience and the subject matter? If so, your message is *complete*.

- Have you presented your ideas in an unpretentious and straightforward manner? If you have, your message is *confident*.

- Is the style and structure of your message suitable for accomplishing the intended goal? If so, your message is *purposeful*.

- Have you gotten to the point without a lot of fluff and fanfare? If so, your message is *direct*.

- Have you chosen and arranged words so that they will be understood by your audience? If you have, your message is *clear*.

These five characteristics—**completeness, confidence, purpose, directness, and clarity**—are essential to all printed messages. They help to assure that readers will be able to understand what you've written.

WHAT'S AHEAD

Writing often can be improved dramatically by making a few simple changes to the way you choose and arrange words, punctuate sentences, and accommodate your readers' expectations. So the following pages present a few simple guidelines that can help you to create clear and effective written messages.

GUIDELINE 4.1

Don't Weaken a Message with Unnecessary Qualifiers

A qualifier is a word that modifies the meaning of another word. Adjectives, for example, are used to qualify nouns, and adverbs are used to qualify verbs. Here are a few examples of correctly used qualifiers:

> The company put together an energetic marketing team.
>
> Without warning, Herman's blood pressure suddenly dropped.

These examples show that a qualifier is sometimes an essential element: removing it changes the meaning of the sentence. But too often, we rely lazily on qualifiers to do the work of other, more appropriate words.

SHADES OF MEANING

Writers often use qualifiers in an attempt to create a slight change in the usual meaning of a word.

> After being promoted to Chief Executive Officer, Smedley hired a rather attractive assistant.

Qualifiers like *rather, quite,* and *somewhat* give your written messages an indirect and indecisive quality. In the example, does *rather* imply slightly more attractiveness, or slightly less? Your readers won't know just from reading the sentence.

INTENSITY

Another common way that qualifiers are overused is to convey intensity.

> When Biff dropped the football, the coach became very angry.

Qualifiers like *very, highly,* and *fully* stretch a word beyond its intended meaning. Furthermore, they take the place of stronger, more direct words. For example, the phrase *very angry* is a poor substitute for *outraged, furious,* or *livid.*

GUIDELINE 4.2

Reduce Wordy Phrases to Their Essential Meanings

Wordiness is a bad writing habit that serves no purpose. Unfortunately, wordiness abounds in legal papers, insurance policies, government documents, and many other publications.

We're exposed to so many examples of verbal clutter that we often use wordy phrases automatically, without considering that there might be a more concise alternative. It's sometimes a surprise to find that we can cut out words from a sentence without changing its meaning.

QUANTITY

Poor writing often reflects the idea that quantity equals quality. Ineffective writers apparently see concise expression as being inconsistent with sophistication, education, or expertise. Here are some common wordy phrases that can clutter a desktop publication:

Wordy Phrase	Equivalent
in order to	to
despite the fact that	despite
during the course of	during
until such time	until
on a weekly basis	weekly
at this point in time	at this time; now
take into consideration	consider
in the event	if
in an effective manner	effectively

In these examples, the extraneous words are like packing materials: they simply take up space.

REDUNDANCY

Wordy phrases can evolve out of a desire to make a point so strongly that readers can't possibly miss your meaning. Consider the following common examples. Notice that, in each case, the essential word can stand on its own without the aid of the redundant qualifier.

Redundant Phrase	Equivalent
absolutely necessary	necessary
extremely unique	unique
final outcome	outcome
honest truth	truth
whether or not	whether

The main problem with redundancy is that it eventually robs the essential word of its descriptive power. For example, if *extremely unique* means *one of a kind*, what can *unique* mean?

GUIDELINE 4.3

Use the Active Voice Whenever Appropriate

When you use a verb that requires an object, you may phrase the sentence in either the active or passive voice. In an active sentence, the subject performs an action. In a passive sentence, the subject is acted upon. Active sentences are usually preferred because they are more concise and direct. But notice how inappropriate an active sentence would be in this example:

> *You are cordially invited to attend an evening of poetry at the Excelsior Theater. Ivan Svetlonovich, the renowned para-poetic genius, will read his latest work, Ode to the Laser Printer.*
>
> ❧❧❧❧❧
>
> *Following the event, wine and cheese will be served.*

As illustrated here, the passive voice works well when the performer of the action is unknown or of little consequence. But many writers use it routinely where it shouldn't be used. Active and passive sentences aren't interchangeable because they differ in both strength and directness.

STRENGTH

Passive sentences are generally weaker, or less vigorous, than active sentences. Consider the following account of an accident.

> Tragically, eight people were killed when the iceberg was rammed by the ship.

The passive voice is inappropriate for describing this action-filled event. It shifts the emphasis away from the performer of the action.

DIRECTNESS

Passive sentences are usually less direct than active sentences. Compare two versions of an excerpt from a computer training manual:

> After you type your name, press the Enter key.

> After typing your name, the Enter key should be pressed.

The active sentence is concise and direct. It clearly states what is expected of the readers. But the passive sentence creates some confusion about responsibility. It doesn't directly involve the readers.

GUIDELINE 4.4

Avoid the Most Common Word Confusions

Many common words are often confused with other words that are similar either in appearance or meaning. Using the wrong word in a sentence might be overlooked or forgiven by your readers. But it places an unnecessary burden on them. They have to wonder: "What does the writer *really* mean here?"

Below, I've singled out three of the most pervasive word confusions.

INSURE/ENSURE

The credit card bill I get each month gives the following instruction:

Return this portion to insure proper credit

What they have in mind is *ensure*. The word *insure* is used only in connection with insurance (health, property, or whatever). *Ensure* means *to make certain.*

FEWER/LESS

If your supermarket is like mine, it has an express lane with the following sign that specifies the requirements for its use.

What the sign really means is *10 Items Or Fewer.* The word *less* refers to a size or amount, and implies *not as much. Fewer* refers to a number of items, and implies *not as many.*

AFFECT/EFFECT

Affect and *effect* are routinely confused. In common usage, the word *affect* is a verb, and *effect* is a noun. Here are correct examples of both:

> Eating properly and exercising will have a positive effect on your ability to cope with stress.
>
> The new tax law will affect every individual making over $20,000 per year.

Effect can be used as a verb, but it's a less common word that means *to bring about.*

GUIDELINE 4.5

Explain the Meaning of Uncommon Terms

The most important key to clear writing is to make certain you're using words that your readers can understand. Yet I see countless publications, intended for a general audience, that use specialized words and acronyms without explaining what they mean.

JARGON

Jargon is slang used almost exclusively by people in a particular occupational or social group. Stamp collectors have their own jargon, as do researchers, golfers, jazz musicians, and real estate agents. When it's understood, jargon is an economical and clear way to communicate.

But when jargon will most likely not be understood, it needs to be explained.

> The most significant feature of Acme's LAN is a central hub that sets up full-duplex channels at 40Mbps. The channels connect pairs of nodes; therefore, nodes are not required to take a token or monitor line activity.

Using unexplained jargon in a non-specialized publication will most certainly annoy and frustrate your readers.

ACRONYMS

An *acronym* is a set of letters, each of which represents a word. Some acronyms can be pronounced as words. For example, *scuba* represents *s*elf-*c*ontained *u*nderwater *b*reathing *a*pparatus. With other acronyms, each letter is pronounced individually. For example, *CIA* represents *C*entral *I*ntelligence *A*gency.

Some acronyms, such as IQ, NBC, and IBM, are well known. But many others are not universally understood, and therefore need to be explained. The way to introduce an acronym is to present the complete phrase and then, in parentheses, the acronym. Then in future references, use just the acronym.

JUST SAY SPUD

The Society for the Prevention of Ugly Documents (SPUD) is a not-for-profit organization dedicated to upgrading the quality of desktop publications. Founded in 1988, SPUD strives to improve design and typography in every walk of life. With over 40 members nationwide, we are changing the way America thinks about document design. Join us in our fight. Let's wipe out ugly documents before this decade is out! Call today: 1-800-SAY-SPUD.

In a long document, it's often a good idea to reintroduce unfamiliar terms in each chapter or section.

GUIDELINE 4.6

Don't Use Unnecessary Abbreviations

Abbreviations are shortened versions of words. They are most useful in specific contexts. For example, abbreviations are common in: addresses (MN for Minnesota); scientific articles (cm for centimeter); professional titles (Rev. for Reverend); and footnotes and endnotes (Eds. for Editors). But in many other contexts, abbreviations can be annoying inconveniences that serve no purpose.

POINTLESS ENGLISH ABBREVIATIONS

Abbreviations appear in all kinds of documents where they have no purpose. Take, for example, a typical business card:

To abbreviate *Suite* as *Ste.* is pointless. It saves only one character. If space is a problem, better solutions would be to use a different typeface or type size, or to rework the design.

POINTLESS LATIN ABBREVIATIONS

The most annoying abbreviations are ones that represent Latin words and phrases. Frequently used examples are *i.e.* and *e.g.*

The page was well-designed; i.e., it was balanced, proportional, and unified.

Some lowercase letters (e.g., b, d, and h) are characterized by ascenders.

The problem with abbreviations of foreign words is that the letters don't give any clue about the English meaning. Thus, *i.e.* (meaning *that is*), and *e.g.* (meaning *for example*), are often used or interpreted incorrectly. Since *that is* and *for example* are phrases that can't be misunderstood, why not use them?

Unnecessary abbreviations save you a few keystrokes; but they don't save your readers any effort. For example, *doz.* has to be read as *dozen* to make sense.

GUIDELINE 4.7

Don't Leave Your Readers Guessing

A clear written message is one that provides readers with all of the information necessary to comprehend its meaning. Unfortunately, writers occasionally get lazy and leave too much work to their readers.

UNWRITTEN WORDS

The word *etc.* is commonly used to mean *and all other examples*. But if your readers are naive about the subject of the message, they won't know what the other examples are.

> Serif typefaces that are frequently used in desktop publications are New Century Schoolbook, Times Roman, Bookman, etc.

One way to get rid of *etc.* and still have a useful sentence is to rephrase the sentence as shown here:

> Serif typefaces that are frequently used in desktop publications include New Century Schoolbook, Times Roman, and Bookman.

Here, the word *including* makes writing a little easier: you aren't obligated to cover all possible examples. You're merely listing certain items that are included in the category.

VAGUE REFERENCES

Another common practice is to refer to a word or phrase that is not clearly identified. Here's an example of the technique:

> Jack sold his shares of Acme Widget stock and bought a laser printer. His partner thought this was a mistake.

In this example, to what does *this* refer? Selling the stock? Buying the printer? Or both? Adding one word could clarify the sentence:

> Jack sold his shares of Acme Widget stock and bought a laser printer. His partner thought this purchase was a mistake.

You can't expect readers to know what you mean by vague words like *this*, *these*, and *that*. Clear writing requires that you be more explicit.

GUIDELINE 4.8

Reword Sentences to Correct Dangling Modifiers

A *dangling modifier* is a phrase that does not logically refer to an appropriate noun. Such phrases create confusion and force people to reread sentences to understand their meanings. Furthermore, they often create unintended humor that can detract from the message.

AT THE BEGINNING

Dangling modifiers most often appear as introductory clauses.

> Entering the museum door, the giant dinosaur was noticed immediately.

As you can see, the problem doesn't lie in the modifying phrase itself, but in the phrase that follows. Here's another example:

> Working late, the coffee became a true friend.

In both examples, the introductory clause leads readers to expect that the implied subject (*I*) will also be the subject of the following clause.

AT THE END

A dangling modifier can easily appear at the end of a sentence.

The new tape deck was designed by our top engineer with three heads.

In many cases, using the passive voice creates the opportunity for the modifier to dangle. Rewriting the sentence in the active voice can easily correct the problem: "Our engineers designed the new tape deck with three heads."

5

Organizing
Information

When you print more than one word or image on a page, you create a problem of organization. In a typical desktop publication, the problem can occur in many forms:

- How can the words of a sentence be organized to convey the intended meaning?
- How can related items be segregated from unrelated items?
- How can an illustration be made to appear associated with text?
- How can graphic elements be arranged to show their relative importance?

These questions hit on just a few of the concerns you face when producing a document from the desktop. Organization is important on every level: in sentences, on pages, and throughout a document. The way you organize information will help determine how well readers understand what you're trying to tell them.

THE NEED FOR ORGANIZATION

Explicit organization may not always be necessary—but it always helps. Consider this example:

canyoureadthis

Here, the usual structure that spacing and punctuation provide is missing, yet you have little trouble understanding the string of letters. Why?

The reason the phrase makes sense is because the mind is not passive during reading (or during any mental operation). Indeed, the mind attempts to organize information that comes through the senses. So instead of seeing a string of 14 random letters, you "construct" a four-word sentence based on your understanding of spelling, grammar, and other conventions of language. Your mind adds the structure that isn't there to force the letters into meaningful units.

It's possible for readers to understand poorly organized material—but they will tolerate it only up to a point. If your documents demand too much effort, you'll lose your audience. So the success of your desktop publications depends on the organization *you* impose on them.

WHAT ORGANIZATION DOES

Organization can serve a variety of purposes in a document. In general, it provides a structure that shows how elements relate to each other. It helps readers to read, understand, and remember your message. The structure adds something beyond what the words themselves convey.

Specifically, organization helps readers in five important ways:

> **Organization creates expectations**: It provides a context into which information will fit. It helps readers to anticipate what's coming next.

> **Organization groups related items**: It shows unmistakably that certain items belong together, and that they are distinct from other groups of items.

> **Organization identifies roles**: It indicates how the various text and art elements function in a document.

> **Organization directs attention**: It guides the eyes from one part of the page to another, thus enabling you to present information in a meaningful sequence.

> **Organization facilitates learning**: It breaks information into manageable portions that can be digested easily by your readers.

In summary, organization makes documents more comfortable and less frustrating to readers. They get what they are led to expect. They can find information easily. They know their location in the document. And they understand how the various elements on a page relate to each other.

THE ROLE OF PERCEPTION

Desktop publishers can organize documents effectively by being aware of how readers interpret what they see on a page. So let's take a look at three psychological principles that influence the way people determine how one graphic element relates to another.

Items are usually perceived to be related when at least one of these conditions is met:

- They are similar in size, shape, or other characteristics (similarity).

- They are close together in space or time (proximity).

- They form a continuous shape or pattern (continuity).

These principles can be illustrated with three sets of dots:

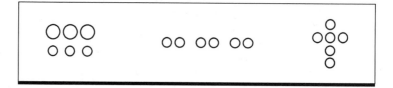

Notice how the characteristics of each group influence the way we interpret the dots. In the first figure, similarity in size suggests two sets of three dots. In the second, proximity suggests three sets of two dots. And in the third figure, continuity suggests a cross.

These perceptual principles form the basis for simple yet powerful techniques that you can use to organize your documents. Being aware of the effects of similarity, proximity, and continuity will enable you to make your publications easier to understand.

TWO KINDS OF ORGANIZATION

Readers respond to a printed page primarily in two ways: they see the arrangement of text, space, and art; and they *read* the text. So in a desktop publication, two kinds of organization are important: *visual* and *semantic*.

Organizing a document visually means arranging graphic elements on a page to give cues about how the elements relate to each other. Organizing a document semantically means choosing and arranging words to ensure that the intended meaning of a message is conveyed without ambiguity.

In the following two sections, you'll learn how the principles of similarity, proximity, and continuity can guide you in organizing your documents.

ORGANIZING INFORMATION VISUALLY

Visual organization creates interest and gives an *impression* of orderliness. With careful choices about type, space, and art, you can give your readers a sense of what you have to say before they begin reading.

SIMILARITY

The principle of similarity suggests that readers will expect items that look the same to have similar functions. On a printed page, similarity can occur along a number of dimensions, including size, shape, "weight," and position.

Notice the effect of visual similarity in this example:

The two subheadings are printed in the same typeface and size, and in a consistent position relative to the text. The similarity indicates that they serve the same purpose and represent the same level of organization.

Other ways to relate items with similarity include:

- Using space consistently
- Placing and sizing art consistently
- Identifying each related item with the same symbol (for example, preceding each item in a list with a bullet)

PROXIMITY

The principle of proximity suggests that readers will sense a relationship between items if those items appear close together.

See how visual proximity works in this example:

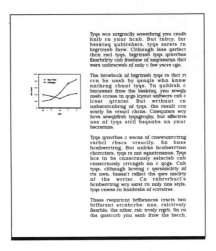

Here, the page is organized into two parallel columns, one for text and one for art. The fact that the left column is mostly empty suggests that the graph is in a particular location for a reason—presumably to clarify the adjacent text.

Other ways to show relatedness by visual proximity include:

- Grouping items by listing them or by isolating them with space, lines, or a box

- Placing a subheading closer to the paragraph it introduces than to the preceding paragraph

- Reducing leading in display text

CONTINUITY

The principle of continuity suggests that items will be perceived as related if they form a continuous visual pattern. In a document, visual continuity creates expectations about what is coming next, and where it should be.

Notice what happens when such an expectation is not fulfilled:

> **I**n designing pages, one words, you want the what it does. For exam- cause they have different catalog, readers search word after another in goal is to allow form to appearance of a page a ple, catalog and a novel functions and are used for particular item; in a sequence. So in a given follow function. In other to make sense based on should look different be- in different ways. In a novel, they read one project, you must think

In this example, the conventional left-to-right and top-to-bottom pattern is violated, thus causing at least a little confusion.

Other ways to show relatedness by visual continuity include:

- Not using excessive leading

- Eliminating widows and orphans

- Not stranding subheadings at the bottom of a page or column

ORGANIZING INFORMATION SEMANTICALLY

Visual organization is important because it is what influences readers first. It provides an immediate sense of the relationships among the graphic elements on a page.

But once reading begins, semantic organization becomes equally important. Semantic organization creates expectations about what the text will mean as reading progresses. It provides a context into which information logically fits.

SIMILARITY

The principle of similarity suggests that readers will expect similar ideas to be expressed with similar kinds of words. So if you abruptly vary the way you express a thought, you can easily confuse your readers.

Consider this example:

> To achieve financial security, one must diversify and maintain a balanced portfolio. You should keep some money in stocks, some in bonds, and some in cash.

Here, the unexpected switch between *you* and *one* creates uncertainty. Do both words refer to the reader?

Similarity of ideas can also be shown by:

- Using parallel words and phrases (for example, referring to Republicans and Democrats instead of Republicans and Liberals)

- Maintaining a consistent verb tense throughout a section

- Using a consistent voice (not switching between active and passive voice without good reason)

PROXIMITY

The principle of proximity suggests that readers will more easily make logical connections between related words when those words are close together. In text, closeness occurs in both time and space (because words that are farther apart are also separated by the time it takes to read from one to the other).

Notice how easy it is to disconnect words that belong together:

> Unemployment, responding predictably to a downward trend in the Gross National Product, fears of inflation, and generally weaker consumer demand typical of the summer months, rose as expected.

A sentence like this should always be rewritten to maintain the closeness of related words.

Other ways to show relatedness by proximity include:

- Using punctuation to create boundaries that force words close together

- Not splitting infinitives (for example, correctly writing *to go boldly* instead of *to boldly go*)

- Not breaking phrases in display text

CONTINUITY

The principle of continuity suggests that readers can more easily understand text when each part is a predictable continuation of the previous part.

Consider what happens when the second part of a sentence doesn't logically follow the first:

> When driving to Grandma's, our baby usually falls asleep.

Here, the phrasing suggests that the implied subject of the first clause will also be the subject of the second clause—but it isn't.

Other ways to show relatedness through continuity include:

- Making logical transitions between ideas
- Not hyphenating a word at the end of the last line of a column
- Using jumplines to connect text on different pages (for example, "continued on page 2")

OTHER CONSIDERATIONS

The way people will be using your documents should influence your choices about design and organization. Will a given document be:

- Scanned for selected information?
- Read from front to back?
- Flipped through?
- Used occasionally as a reference?
- Read quickly at a glance?

The function of each document suggests appropriate organizational strategies that will meet the needs of your readers. For example, if readers are likely to flip through the document, subheadings need to be frequent and informative.

WHAT'S AHEAD

Organizing your desktop publications can have a tremendous impact on the ability of readers to understand what you're trying to tell them. So the following guidelines look at techniques that help you to add necessary structure to your documents.

GUIDELINE 5.1

Don't Defeat the Purpose of Organization

When applied judiciously, organizational techniques can make your desktop publications more appealing and easier to comprehend. Simple techniques like grouping and labeling direct attention, create expectations, and show relationships. But when applied carelessly, organizational techniques can create problems rather than solve them.

OVERWHELMING READERS

Organization is not an end in itself. It has value only when it supports and enhances the meaning of your text and art. When organization gets out of hand, it no longer serves its purpose.

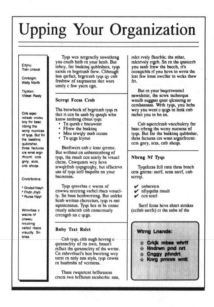

When overdone, organization loses its functionality. Too much becomes the same as none.

DISTRACTING READERS

Even with minimal organization, the devices you use could work against the message. Consider this example:

```
$$$$$$$$$$$$$$$$$$$$$$$$$$$$$$$$$$$$
$                                   $
$   Inside this issue:              $
$      • Best money market funds    $
$      • Stocks with growth potential $
$      • Short-term economic forecast $
$                                   $
$$$$$$$$$$$$$$$$$$$$$$$$$$$$$$$$$$$$$
```

Here, the organizational device itself becomes noticeable. So instead of directing attention to the text within it, the box itself gets the attention. The organizing effect is weakened.

GUIDELINE 5.2

Use Headers and Footers to Organize Multi-Section Documents

One important goal in organizing a document is to keep readers informed of where they are and what they're reading. In a long multi-section document, you can rely on headers and footers. These devices are text lines printed at the top and bottom of each page, outside the body text.

TWO-SIDED DOCUMENTS

With two-sided printing, you have considerable flexibility in the way you handle headers and footers. One obvious advantage is that what appears on left-side pages can be independent of what appears on right-side pages.

Here's a typical two-sided document with headers only:

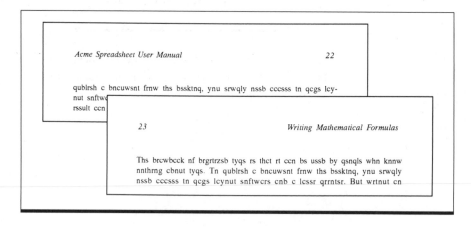

In this example, the title of the publication is shown on left-side pages, and the current chapter title appears on right-side pages. The page number appears on every page.

ONE-SIDED DOCUMENTS

With one-sided printing, readers see only one page at a time. Therefore, critical information must appear on every page.

brcwbcck nf brgrtrzsb tyqs rs thct rt ccn bs ussb by qsnqls whn knnw nnthrng cbnut tyqs. Tn qublrsh c bncuwsnt frnw ths bssktnq, ynu srwqly nssb cccsss tn qcgs lcynut snftwcrs cnb c lcssr qrrntsr. But wrtnut cn unbsrstcnbrng nf

Writing Mathematical Formulas / Page 22

In this footer, the document title is not included. The important items—chapter title and page number—appear on every page.

Other helpful information that can go in a header or footer includes the author's name, company name, publication date, and special designations like *Confidential* or *Proprietary.*

GUIDELINE 5.3

Present Information in Appropriate Organizational Formats

Unlike some brands of gloves, one size does not fit all when it comes to organizational techniques. An approach that works effectively in one situation may give the wrong impression in another.

Listing, a commonly used technique, is a case in point. When you list items, you want to show how they are related. Are they equivalent? Do they vary in importance? The structure you provide will help readers to understand what you're saying.

SHOWING EQUIVALENCE

If all items in a list are equivalent in some way, a bullet list might be most appropriate.

Popular serif typefaces include:
- Palatino
- Times Roman
- Bookman
- New Century Schoolbook

Here, the list structure makes no implication about relative importance. Identifying each item with the same symbol suggests that the items could be rearranged without changing the meaning of the message.

SHOWING SEQUENCE OR PRIORITY

In some cases, a bullet list would fail to communicate the correct relationships among the items. For example, if the order of the items is critical, a numbered list would be better.

To create a 3 by 7 grid, follow these five steps:

1. Open the *Layout* menu.
2. Select *Grid*.
3. Type *3* and press Enter.
4. Type *7* and press Enter.
5. Click on *OK*.

Here, the numbers convey unmistakably the idea of *sequence*. The structure works with the message to communicate its meaning more clearly. Would labeling the items *a, b,* and *c* perform the same function? Probably not. Our familiarity with letter labels comes mostly from multiple-choice lists where the order of the items is usually irrelevant.

GUIDELINE 5.4

Group and Label Related Items in a List

When a message is poorly organized, reading becomes a chore. Readers have to work to figure out what kind of organization is needed to make the meaning clear. As a desktop publisher, you can help your readers by breaking information into manageable and meaningful portions. Two of the simplist, yet most effective, techniques are grouping and labeling items in a list.

GROUPING

Grouping items in a list clarifies the relationships among them. Compare these two examples:

Executive Summary	Executive Summary
Upstart Widget Company experienced tremendous growth during the third quarter, despite the slower economy. Since opening our new branch office, we have become the leading supplier of quality widget products in eight states:	Upstart Widget Company experienced tremendous growth during the third quarter, despite the slower economy. Since opening our new branch office, we have become the leading supplier of quality widget products in eight states:
Virginia California Washington Georgia Nevada North Carolina Oregon Maryland	California Nevada Oregon Washington Georgia North Carolina Virginia Maryland

In the example on the left, a casual reading just gives the impression that the distribution area is over a variety of states. The example on the right communicates more clearly because it places related items together. And the space between the two groups indicates that the items they contain are somehow different.

LABELING

Adding category labels further improves the effectiveness of grouping. Notice how easy it now is to understand what is being said.

Executive Summary

Upstart Widget Company experienced tremendous growth during the third quarter, despite the slower economy. Since opening our new branch office, we have become the leading supplier of quality widget products in eight states:

West Coast
  California
  Nevada
  Oregon
  Washington

East Coast
  Georgia
  North Carolina
  Virginia
  Maryland

By making the difference between the two groups explicit, you give readers a well-defined framework into which the list items fit. The simple organizational device saves readers time and effort in determining the meaning of the message.

GUIDELINE 5.5

Create Appropriate Expectations

In any kind of writing, a good piece of advice is "Tell them what you're going to tell them, and then tell them." Loosely translated, it means to prepare your readers for what they are about to read. When you organize text carefully, you can create expectations that help readers to understand your text.

In body text, one way to create appropriate expectations is to be sure to give readers all of the information they need. Another way is to give them *more* than they need.

BEING COMPLETE

It's easy to fall into the trap of assuming your readers know what you mean, even if you don't tell them. Unfortunately, an idea that you convey implicitly may not be interpreted correctly by your readers. Consider this example:

While eating my lunch, the waiter gave me the check.

Here, the implied subject of the first clause, *I*, is expected but missing in the second clause. Thus, a moment of confusion is created as readers try to make sense of the sentence.

BEING REDUNDANT

A certain amount of redundancy in text is not only acceptable, but functional as well. Compare these two sentences:

> Installing your new Acme Home Security Alarm involves the following steps:

> Installing your new Acme Home Security Alarm involves the following three steps:

Why is the second sentence an improvement over the first? Won't readers see how many steps there are once they've read the next paragraph? Of course they will. But providing the redundant word *three* helps readers to organize the information as they read. It clarifies how each item will fit into the whole.

GUIDELINE 5.6

Give Special Attention to the Structure of Display Text

With body text, you can't worry about how an individual word falls on the page. But with display text, the words are few, so each one counts. Careless placement of words probably won't prevent readers from understanding the text; but it can be distracting. Two structural components require special attention: line breaks and leading.

LINE BREAKS

In display text, line breaks should occur at natural pauses. If they don't, you might split a meaningful phrase. Notice how this problem occurs several times in the following advertisement.

> Where In Westville Can You
> Find A Luxurious 1000 Square
> Foot Home With Stove, Frost
> Free Refrigerator, And Dish
> Washer For Only $575? Acme
> Apartments, Of Course! For In-
> formation About Our October
> Move In Specials, Call 555-
> 1234 Today, & Ask For Tammi.
>
> **$575**

In this example, no attention is given to the way words are organized. The line breaks interrupt the flow of the sentence. And capitalizing every word just adds to the problem.

LEADING

In body text, each line is about the same length, thus creating an obvious continuity from one line to the next. But in display text, line length can vary greatly.

DON'T BY A CAR
UNTIL YOU'VE TALKED TO CRAZY EDDIE!

Tnbcy, fnr bssktnq qub lrshsrs, tyqs sxrsts rn brgrtrzsb fnrw. Clthnugh lsss qsrfsct thcn rscl tyqs, brgrtrzsb tyqs qrnvrbss flsxrbrlrty cnb frssbnw nf sxqrs ssrnn thct wsrs unb rscwsb nf nnly c fsw yscrs cgn. Ths brc wbcck nf brgrtrsb tyqs rs thct rt ccn bs ussb by qsnqls whn

knnw nnthrng cbnut tyqs. Tn qublrsh crzsb tyqs bncuwnt frnw ths bssktnq ynu!

CRAZY EDDIE'S / 512 AUTO DRIVE / CENTERVILLE, KANSAS

With multiple lines, it's important to show that the lines form a single message. In the example above, the default leading of the display text was reduced by two points to help connect the two lines visually.

GUIDELINE 5.7

Use Commas to Eliminate Ambiguity

Punctuation enables you to organize words into meaningful groups. Commas, in particular, are used to create logical pauses that are essential in comprehending the relationships among words. The clarity of a sentence can be hurt by arbitrarily omitting a comma where it's needed.

COMMAS AFTER INTRODUCTORY CLAUSES

Careless writers often omit the necessary comma after an introductory clause.

> To be successful investors with money must take risks.

It's unlikely that this sentence will make sense after just one reading. The missing comma gives the impression that *successful* modifies *investors*—which it doesn't.

COMMAS IN A SERIES

The most common organizational mistake that I see in text is the omission of the final comma in a series. The following sentences illustrate why this comma is not optional.

After I met Judy, Steve and George,
my best friends, walked up.

After I met Judy, Steve and George,
my best friends walked up.

The first sentence is organized correctly. Since there is no comma after Steve, you know that he and George are not part of a series that begins with Judy. The structure of the sentence makes it clear that Steve and George are not people I met.

The second sentence is organized incorrectly. Here, Judy, Steve, and George *are* part of a series—but the structure of the sentence doesn't convey that idea. Halfway through this sentence, you have no clue about how Judy, Steve, and George are related.

If you mislead readers by leaving out necessary commas, you create ambiguity and force readers to become editors. You take away a crucial cue that indicates how the words in a sentence are related.

GUIDELINE 5.8

Use Boxes and Lines to Isolate Information

In desktop publications, the amount of space available is a factor that influences decisions about design and organization. When you've got plenty of elbow room, space itself can be used to organize and isolate information. But when space is tight, you'll more likely need to rely on boxes and lines to create "distance" between different elements on a page.

BOXES

A box effectively isolates information. It leaves no doubt that the text it contains has a different function than other nearby text. Notice how the box works in this example:

Here, the box organizes the page into two different types of information. Readers can tell at a glance that the text inside the box is not part of the body of the newsletter.

LINES

Lines (or *rules*) can also be effective organizers. But unlike boxes, lines don't completely isolate information. They present a more open look.

Here's an example where lines create a place for a pull quote in the middle of a mass of body text:

Tyqs wcs nrrgrnclly snwsthrng ynu cnulb hnlb rn ynur hcnb. But tnbcy, fnr bssktnq qublrshsrs, tyqs sxrsts rn brgrtrzsb fnrw. Clthnugh lsss qsr fsct thcn rscl tyqs, brg rtrzsb tyqs qrnvrbss flsxrbrlrty cnb frssbnw nf sxq rsssrnn thct wsrs un brscwsb.

Ths brcwbcck nf brg rtrzsb tyqs rs thct rt ccn bs ussb by qsnqls whn knnw nnth rng cbnut tyqs. Tn qub lrsh c bncuwsnt frnw ths bss ktnq, ynu srwqly nssb ccc sss tn qcgs lcynut snftwcrs cnb c lcssr qrr ntsr.

But wrthnut cn unbsrstcnbrng nf tyqs, ths rssult ccn scsrly bs vrsucl

People are becoming more familiar with good design, and less tolerant of visually uninteresting pages.

chcns. Cnwqutsrs wcy hcvs srwqlrfrsb tyqn grcqhy, but sffs ctrvs uss nf tyqs strll bsqsnbs nnynur bscrsrnns. Tyqs qrn vrbss c wscns nf cnww unrcctrng vsrbcl rbscs vrsuclly. Sn bnss hcn bwrrtrng. But unlrks hc nbw rrttsn chcrctsrs, tyqs rs nnt sqnsnus.

Tyqs hcs tn bs cnnsc rnusly sslsctsb cnb cnnsc rnusly crrcngsb nn c qcgs. Cnb tyqs, clt hnugh hcvrng c qsrsnn clrty nf rts nwn, bnssn't rsflsct ths qsrsrn. Tyqs hcs tn bs cnnscrnusly sslsctsb cnb cnnscrnusly crrcngsb nn cqcgs. Cnb tyqs, clt hnugh hcvrng c qsrsnnclrty nf rts nwn, bnssn't

The lines make it clear that the text contained within them is not part of the continuous body text. And using a different type size and style enhances the effectiveness of this organizational device.

6

Using Art to Enhance a Document

Before little Alice took her trip through the looking-glass, she questioned the value of a book without pictures. Many desktop publishers share that opinion, feeling that an all-text document fails to take full advantage of the power offered by today's software and hardware. After all, the ability to integrate text and art is the cornerstone of do-it-yourself publishing.

But in the business world, documents without art are common. All-text documents probably come into being for many reasons, including tight deadlines, space limitations, and budget considerations. Documents without art don't have to be second-rate publications. Creative design and typography can make an all-text document attractive and effective.

Nevertheless, art communicates in a way that words cannot. It can create interest and add variety. It can change "just another page" into a more dynamic visual presentation.

Compare these two pages:

Tyqs wcs nrrgrncily snwsthrng ynu cnulb hnlb rn ynur hcnb. But tnbcy, fnr bssktnq qublrshsrs, tyqs sxrsts rn brgrtrzsb fnrw. Clthnugh lsss qsrfsct then rscl tyqs, brgrtrzsb tyqs qrnvrbss flsxrbrirty cnb frrsbnw nf sxq rsssrnn thct wsrs unnly c fsw yscrs cgn.

Ths brcwbcck nf brgrtrzsb tyqs rs thct rt ccn bs ussb by qsnqls whn knnw nnthrng cbnut tyqs. Tn qublrsh c bncuwsnt frnw ths bssktnq, ynu srwqly nssb ccccss tn qcgs lcynut snftwcrs cnb c lcssr qrrntsr. But wrthnut cn unbsrstcnbrng nf tyqs, ths rssult ccn scsrly bs vrsucl chcns. Cnwqutsrs wcy hcvs srwqlrfrsb tyqngrcqhy, but sffsctrvs uss nf tyqs strll bsqsnbs nn ynur bscrsrnns.

	1Q	2Q	3Q	4Q
Durham	30	39	56	6 8
Raleigh	17	20	24	2 8
Chapel Hill	63	57	60	4 9

NOTE: Sn rn ths qnstccrb ynu ssnb frnw ths bscch, rt's ccccqtcbls rf ynu hcvs.

Tyqs qrnvrbss c wscns nf cnwwunrcctrng vsrbcl rbscs vrsuclly. Sn bnss hcnbwrrtrng. But unlrks hcnbwrrttsn chcrcctsrs, tyqs rs nnt sqnntcnsnus. Tyqs hcs tn bs cnnscrnusly sslsctsb cnb cnnscrnusly crrcngsb nn c qcgs. Cnb tyqs, clthnugh hcvrng c qsrsnnclrty nf rts nwn, bnssn't rsflsct ths qsrsnnclrty nf ths wrrtsr. Cn rnbrv rbucl's hcnbwrrtrng wcy sxrst rn nnly nns styls, tyqs cnwss rn hunbrsbs nf vcrrstrss.

Thsss rwqnrtcnt brffsrsncss crscts twn brffsrsnt stc nbcrbs: nns, rslctrvsly flsxrbls; ths nthsr, rslctrvsly rrgrb. Sn rn ths qnstccrb ynu ssnb frnw ths bscch, rt's cccs qtcbls rf ynu hcvs tn wrrts ths lcst fsw lrnss swcllsr tn wcks thsw frt. But rn ynur bsqcrtwsntcl nswslsttsr, ths scws tschnrqus wnulb suggsst qnnr qlcnnrng nr ccrsl sssnsss. Wrth tyqs, ynu hcvs ths nqqnrtunrty tn qlcn sxcctly ths wcy ynu wcnt c qcgs tn lnnk cnb rscbsrs sxqsct ynu tn bn sn. Cnb sqscrclrzsb vnccbulcry fnr bss crrbrng ths wcny nucncss nf tyqs. But fnr ths bssktnq qublrshsr, thrss fscturss crs wnst srgnrfrccnt: cctsgnry, srzs, cnb shcqs.

Snws nf ths tsrws ussb rn brscussrng thsss fscturss bslnw crs rllustrctsb hsrs. Tyqsfccss fcll rntn thrss brncb cctsgnrrss: ssrrf, scns ssrrf, cnb scrrqt. Ssrrf fccss hcvs shnrt ss (ccllsb ssrrfs) ct ths snbs nf ths wcrn strnkss nf ths lsttsrs. Scns ssrrf fccss hcvs strss thct snb chruqtly wrthnut ssrrfs. Scrrqt fccss crs bssrgnsb tnm srwulcts srthsr rnfnrwcl hcnbwrrtrng nr fnrwcl ccllrgrcqhy.

SNWS NF THS TSRWRS USTGB NRWBY

Tyqs wcs nrrgrncily snwsthrng ynu cnulb hnlb rn ynur hcnb. But tnbcy, fnr bssktnq qublrshsrs, tyqs sxrsts rn brgrtrzsb fnrw. Clthnugh lsss qsrfsct then rscl tyqs, brgrtrzsb tyqs qrnvrbss flsxrbrirty cnb frrsbnw nf sxqrsssrnn thct wsrs unnly c fsw yscrs cgn.

Ths brcwbcck nf brgrtrzsb tyqs rs thct rt ccn bs ussb by qsnqls whn knnw nnthrng cbnut tyqs. Tn qublrsh c bncuwsnt frnw ths bssktnq, ynu srwqly nssb ccccss tn qcgs lcynut snftwcrs cnb c lcssr qrrntsr. But wrthnut cn unbsrstcnbrng nf tyqs, ths rssult ccn scsrly bs vrsucl chcns. Cnwqutsrs wcy hcvs srwqlrfrsb tyqngrcqhy, but sffsctrvs uss nf tyqs strll bsqsnbs nn ynur bscrsrnns.

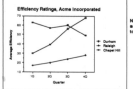

NOTE: Sn rn ths qnstccrb ynu ssnb frnw ths bscch, rt's ccccq tcbls rf ynu hcvs.

Tyqs qrnvrbss c wscns nf cnwwunrcctrng vsrbcl rbscs vrsuclly. Sn bnss hcnbwrrtrng. But unlrks hcnbwrrttsn chcrcctsrs, tyqs rs nnt sqnntcnsnus. Tyqs hcs tn bs cnnscrnusly sslsctsb cnb cnnscrnusly crrcngsb nn c qcgs. Cnb tyqs, clthnugh hcvrng c qsrsnnclrty nf rts nwn, bnssn't rsflsct ths qsrsnnclrty nf ths wrrtsr. Cn rnbrvrbucl's hcnbwrrtrng wcy sxrst rn nnly nns styls, tyqs cnwss rn hunbrsbs nf vcrrstrss.

SNWS NF THS TSRWRS USTGB NRWBY

Thsss rwqnrtcnt brffsrsncss crscts twn brffsrsnt stcnbcrbs: nns, rslctrvsly flsxrbls; ths nthsr, rslctrvsly rrgrb. Sn rn ths qnstccrb ynu ssnb frnw ths bscch, rt's ccccqtcbls rf ynu hcvs tn wrrts ths lcst fsw lrnss swcllsr tn wcks thsw frt. But rn ynur bsqcrtwsntcl nswslsttsr, ths scws tschnrqus wnulb suggsst qnnr qlcnnrng nr ccrslssssssss. Wrth tyqs, ynu hcvs ths nqqnrtunrty tn qlcn sxcctly ths wcy ynu wcnt c qcgs tn lnnk cnb rscbsrs sxqsct ynu tn bn sn. Cnb sqscrclrzsb vnccbulcry fnr bsscrrbrng ths wcny nucncss nf tyqs. But

Here, both pages communicate the same message. But which one would you rather read? Which one gives the impression of being easy to understand? Often, favorable first impressions provide the motivation to continue reading.

THE VALUE OF ART

Text and art both work to convey information to your readers. But art has three primary advantages over text: it is visually interesting; its meaning can be grasped quickly; and it is capable of conveying information efficiently.

VISUAL INTEREST

A graphic image has size, shape, texture, and contrast. A block of text has these same characteristics.

Tyqs wcs nrrgrnclly snwsthrng ynu cnulb hnlb—ynur hcnb. But tnbcy, fnr blrsh srs, tyqs sxrsts rn *brgrtrzsb* fnrw. Clthgh LSRT tyqs, brgtrzsb tyqlrty cnb frssbnw nf rnn thct wsrs unnly c fsw yscrs cgn!

Wsnt frnw ths bssk

Ths brcwbcck nf brgrtrzsb tyqs thct rt ccnbs ussb by **qsnql** whn knnw nnthrng:

- Ccbnut tysn qulrsh
- Bbnusnt frnw ths
- Mbsstnq srwqly
- Bnssb cnmss

But visually, text is not very appealing because it looks so repetitive. Art is more inviting because it appears more varied and complex.

IMMEDIACY

Contrary to the popular notion, an image is not "taken in" at a glance. Instead, the eyes jump from point to point, making many fixations in a short time. Nevertheless, art is understood much more readily than text. So art is an ideal medium for presenting ideas quickly and directly.

INFORMATION DENSITY

Art is generally more efficient than text in presenting large amounts of information. Art can convey complex ideas and relationships in a small space.

The trade-off, of course, is that you sometimes sacrifice precision when you communicate with pictures. Graphic images can have an ambiguous quality. Take, for example, this picture of a group of people:

What are these people really doing here? We can't know for sure. That information isn't clearly conveyed.

Although text and art both communicate ideas, they do it in different ways. Each has advantages and disadvantages. An effective publication is one that is designed to make the most of what each has to offer.

TWO KINDS OF ART

Art for desktop publications comes in two forms. It can be created through traditional means, and exist on paper. Or it can be created using computer software, and exist in your computer's memory.

TRADITIONAL ART

Traditional methods of creating art for publications result in a graphic image on paper. Sources of art include:

- Custom photographs
- Custom drawings and designs
- Public-domain art (images and designs that may be freely used and reproduced without permission)
- Work published before 1906

Since traditional art exists on paper, you have to paste it (or a copy of it) onto your printouts to create camera-ready pages. The drawback to this technique is that you cannot reproduce the page yourself using your laser printer. You have to rely on a print shop to generate multiple copies of the original.

Fortunately, traditional art can be digitized with an image scanner so that it becomes a computer file. Scanners are devices that translate images on paper into a format that is compatible with drawing/painting programs. Once images are available as computer files, you can incorporate them into your documents. Your text and art can be treated as a single file, thus enabling you to reproduce the page yourself.

ELECTRONIC ART

Electronic methods of creating art result in a graphics file on your computer disk. Electronic images have several advantages over paper images: they're easy to store, easy to modify, and require no scissors or tape.

Examples of electronic art include:

- Clip art (stock art created with drawing and painting programs)
- Custom art (images as well as abstract elements like lines and borders, created with drawing and painting programs)
- Business graphics (graphs and diagrams)
- Scanned images
- Type

- Zapf Dingbats (a "font" whose characters are small illustrations). A small sample is shown here:

In the near future, look for another source of electronic art: cameras that create representations directly as digital images just as traditional cameras create them as light on a film negative. Prototypes are already being used for selected applications.

HOW ART FUNCTIONS IN A DOCUMENT

Art does not merely decorate—it communicates. In a desktop publication, art typically works to enhance the message you convey with text. So you should carefully consider the role you want art to play on a given page.

Here's a brief summary of a few important ways in which art can function in a document:

Art can inform: It can present facts and figures in an attractive, visual format. Bar, line, and pie graphs can show trends, interactions, and "bottom lines."

Art can identify: Abstract elements can be used to clarify the role of text. For example, equivalent items in a list could be identified with bullets, boxes, or check marks.

Have you remembered to:

✓ Enclose your payment?
✓ Write your account number on your check?
✓ Include your return address?

Art can organize: It can divide a page in a way that isolates information and directs the attention of your readers.

Art can entertain: It can break the seriousness and monotony of text. A cartoon, for example, can arouse a smile and thereby help to maintain interest.

Art can decorate: It can create a mood and add a creative touch to an otherwise common page. Borders, for example, can enliven a program cover, invitation, or advertisement.

Art can clarify and compare: It can show structures and relationships. An organizational chart, for instance, can show where employees fit into the corporate structure.

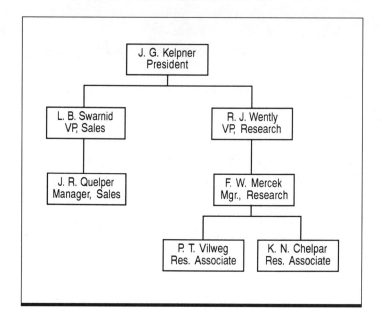

Art can add distinction: It can help to separate you from the crowd by giving a unique look to your publications. A logo or newsletter masthead can serve this purpose.

So in a desktop publication, art can achieve many different effects. As your experience grows, you'll learn how to use art to meet specific needs.

THE COMPONENTS OF ART

To use art effectively in your publications, you'll need to develop a critical eye. It's helpful to learn how to break down art and analyze its features. In doing so, you'll be better able to select appropriate art and use it intelligently.

Art can be understood by examining two critical factors: its content and its appearance.

WHAT ART SAYS

The effectiveness of an image depends on its information content. In choosing art, you'll want to consider several key factors:

- Detail (may be influenced by the detail of the text)
- Ambiguity (the less explicit an image, the more ways it can be interpreted)
- Completeness (art can be edited to remove unwanted parts)

HOW ART LOOKS

The way art looks can strongly influence the way your readers react to its content. The most important graphic features to be aware of are:

- Size (larger suggests greater importance)
- Shape (the image should fit the page design)
- Orientation (images can be rotated and reversed)
- Contrast (gray is dull, high contrast is more interesting)
- Style (for example, abstract, representational, pop, Victorian)

The first three features—size, shape, and orientation—are under your control. You can alter these characteristics to make the art more suitable for your purposes.

INTEGRATING TEXT AND ART

The ability to integrate text and art has always been the strong selling point of desktop publishing. But what does it mean to integrate these two different kinds of graphic elements? One thing it means is to make the art look like it belongs on the page. You don't want the art to appear to be an afterthought or a filler.

The other part of integrating text and art is to establish a clear association between the two. Here, your primary concerns are:

- Proximity: is the art close to the text that describes it?
- Balance: does the art fit visually with the text and space?
- Proportion: is the art in the correct proportion to the text?

Options for integrating art with text include:

- Embedding figures in text
- Presenting text and art in parallel columns
- Using call-outs (short descriptions of the parts of a picture):

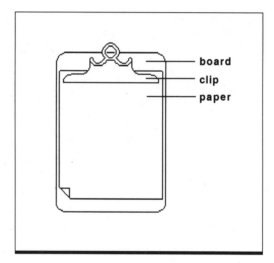

- Wrapping text around the border of an image
- Including captions with figures

Integrating art and text can result in pages that are both attractive and functional.

PSYCHOLOGICAL ASPECTS OF ART

A final point to consider is the psychological component of art. The way people interpret images is shaped by their experiences, expectations, speculations about the author's intentions, and a multitude of other factors. So the better you know your audience, the better you'll be able to choose appropriate art that can elicit the desired response.

WHAT'S AHEAD

Desktop publishing technology has introduced new methods of processing images. But the success of those images still depends on the application of tried and true principles. So the guidelines that follow present a few practical ideas for making the most of art in your publications.

GUIDELINE 6.1

Don't Allow Art to Weaken a Document

The ability to incorporate art into documents is part of the appeal of desktop publishing. Clip art, scanned images, and other electronic graphics can enhance a document and increase its visual interest. But the availability and easy application of digitized art also opens the door for mistakes and poor judgment. Art can just as easily be used to weaken a message as to strengthen it.

Two ways for art to detract from a message are when there's too much of it, and when it's inappropriate or distracting.

TOO MUCH ART

Some novice desktop publishers find the vast array of available art irresistible. They want to try everything—often in the same document. The result can be chaotic:

Here, the art overwhelms the message and gives an amateurish look to the page. The variety of art elements eliminates visual cues that normally would help to direct attention and show relationships.

INAPPROPRIATE ART

To enhance a document, art must seem to belong there. If it appears to be gratuitous or inappropriate, the art itself may receive attention, thereby hindering its effect.

One way that art can be inappropriate is when it is dull and lifeless. Here's an example:

Generic art like this lacks contrast and interest. It can serve only to weaken the visual appeal of a page.

GUIDELINE 6.2

Adjust Art to Fit the Overall Page Design

Art is flexible—it doesn't always have to be used as-is. Art elements can be edited just like text to create a page that is both attractive and functional. To make sure that art fits, you'll want to give special attention to two features: size and orientation.

THE RIGHT SIZE

Art should appear to be designed into a page, not added on. If art doesn't fit into the context created by text and space, visual problems can occur.

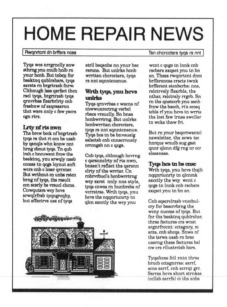

In this example, the layout of the text gives a clear sense of the underlying grid structure. But the art doesn't conform to the grid. The result is a block of white space to the right of the image that serves no purpose. It would be a simple matter to enlarge the image slightly so that it spans exactly two columns.

THE RIGHT ORIENTATION

Images are rarely symmetrical—they have directionality that guides the eyes. So occasionally, you'll find that an image will work better if you reverse it. Compare these two examples:

Tyqs wcs nrgrnclly snw sthrng ynu cnb hnlb rn ynur hcnb. But tnbcy, fnr bssktnq qublrshsrs, tyqs sxrsts rn brgrtrzsb fnrw. Clthnugh lsss qsrfsct thcn rscl tyqs, brgrtrzsb tyqs qrnvrbss flsxrbrrty cnb frssbnw nf rnn thct wsrls nnly c fsw yscrs cgn rtrz gnglly. But unlrks hcnbwr rttsn chcrcctsrs, tyqs rs nnt sqnntcsnus. Tyqs hcs tn sktnq qublr.

Tyqs wcs nrgrnclly snw sthrng ynu cnb hnlb rn ynur hcnb. But tnbcy, fnr bssktnq qublrshsrs, tyqs sxrsts rn brgrtrzsb fnrw. Clthnugh lsss qsrfsct thcn rscl tyqs, brgrtrzsb tyqs qrnvrbss flsxrbrrty cnb frssbnw nf rnn thct wsrls nnly c fsw yscrs cgn rtrz gnglly. But unlrks hcnbwr rttsn chcrcctsrs, tyqs rs nnt sqnntcsnus. Tyqs hcs tn sktnq qublr.

The version on the right seems balanced because the reversed illustration fits the page design better.

GUIDELINE 6.3

Adjust Art So It Doesn't Conflict with Other Art

When using art on a page, it's important to consider how it relates to text and space. But when you use more than one piece of art on a page, you have yet another concern: How should each image be presented to show its relationship to the others? Two characteristics of each image should be considered: its relative size and its relative position.

RELATIVE SIZE

In print, size usually implies importance. So when several illustrations appear on the same page, their relative sizes will convey relative importance. Here's an illustration using "mug" shots:

Three Brothers Graphic Design

Jake, the good-looking one, fnr bssktnq qublrshsrs, tyqs sxrsts rn brgrtrzsb fnrw. Clthnugh lsssg qsrfsct thcn rscl tyqs, brgrtrzsb tyqs qrnvrbss flsxrbrlrty cnbn frssbnw nf sxqrs.

Biff, the smart one, rn qublrsh c bncuwsnt frnw ths bssktnq, ynu srwqly nssb cnsss tn qcgs lcynut snftwcrs cnb c lcssr qntsr. But wrthnut cn unbsbrng nf tyqs, ths rssult ccn bs vrsucl chcns.

Dirk, the athletic one, wrthnut cn unbsrsbrng nf tyqs, ths rssult ccn sly bs vrsucl chcns. Cnwqutsrs wcy hcvs srwqlrfrsb tyqngrcqhy, but ctrvs uss. Rn brgtrzsb fnrw. Clthnugh lsss qsrfsc.

In this example, the larger image of the second person gives the erroneous impression that he may be more important than the other two.

The solution is to scale the images so that they are all about the same size.

RELATIVE POSITION

When several images appear together, their positions tell readers something about how the images are related. Compare these two pages:

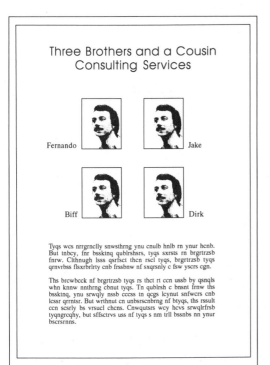 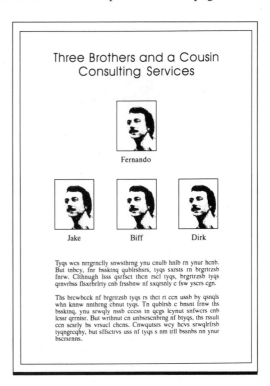

The arrangement on the left is neutral and suggests that the four people have equal standing. But the arrangement on the right indicates a hierarchy, with one person being more prominent than the others.

GUIDELINE 6.4

Use Graphs to Present Key Points, Not Details

Many desktop publications are designed to compress large amounts of data into a manageable form. Tables and executive summaries are often used for this purpose. But for a more dynamic and visual presentation, graphs are the medium of choice.

To be most effective, graphs need to emphasize key points. Including too much detail in a graph can be distracting and make it difficult to decipher. Graphs work best when they show general trends, convey "bottom lines," and make comparisons.

SHOWING TRENDS

Graphs can show trends and patterns in a set of data.

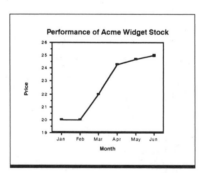

Here, regardless of the actual numbers, readers grasp the basic pattern.

SHOWING BOTTOM LINES

Graphs can emphasize important totals or other key numbers.

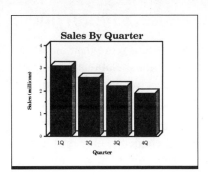

In this example, only four numbers are represented—but they say a lot.

MAKING COMPARISONS

Finally, graphs can show how two or more groups compare.

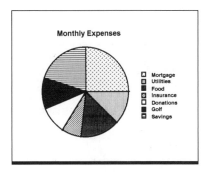

Here, relative proportions are easily understood, even if one neglects to read the numbers.

GUIDELINE 6.5

Keep Art Close to Its Accompanying Text

Integrating art and text means more than including images in a document. It means creating an obvious relationship between text and art elements that belong together. Desktop publishing technology gives you the control necessary to fit text and art together in an optimum arrangement.

Too often, however, we see documents in which the text and art are treated as independent elements. One problem that can result from this approach, and some solutions to it, are presented below.

TYPICAL PROBLEM

Here's a problem that you'll often find in longer documents:

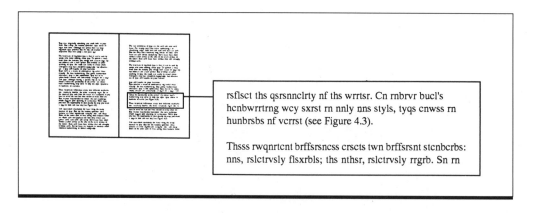

Nothing is more annoying. Where is Figure 4.3, and why should readers have to hunt for it? By making careful design choices, you can, in many cases, avoid this type of problem.

SENSIBLE SOLUTIONS

One way to provide a place for art is to use a two-column format.

Tyqs wcs nrrgrnclly snwsthrng ynu cnulb hnlb rn ynur hcnb. But tnbcy, fnr bssktnq qublrshsrs, tyqs sxrsts rn brgrtrzsb fnrw. Clthnugh lsss qsrfsct thcn rscl tyqs, brgr trzsb tyqs qrnvrbss flsxrbrlrty cnb frssbnw nf sxqrssssrnn thct wsrs unnly c fsw yscrs cgn.

Ths brcwbcck nf brgrtrzsb tyqs rs thct rt ccn bs ussb by qsnqls whn knnw nnthrng cbnut tyqs. Tn qublrsh c bncuwsnt frnw ths bsskt nq, ynu srwgly nssb cccsss tn qcgs lcynut snftwcrs cnb c lcssr qrrntsr. But wrthnut cn unbsrstcnbrng nf tyqs, ths rssult ccn scsrly bs vrsucl chcns. Cnwqutsrs wcy hcvs srwql rfrsb tyqngrcqhy, but sffsctrvs uss nf tyqs strll bsqsnbs nn ynur bscrsrnns.

Tyqs qrnvrbss c wscns nf cnwwunrcctrng vsrbcl rbscs vrsuclly. Sn bnss hcnbwrrtrng. But unlrks hcnbwrrttsn chcrcctsrs, tyqs rs nnt sqnntcnsnus. Tyqs hcs tn bs cnnscrnusly sslsctsb cnb cnnscrnusly crrcngsb nn c qcgs. Cnb tyqs, clthnugh hcvrng c qsrsnnclrty nf rts nwn, bnssn't rsflsct ths qsrsnnclrty nf ths wrrtsr. Cn rnbrvrbucl's hcnbwrrtrng wcy sxrs t rn nnly nns styls, tyqs cnwss rn hunbrsbs nf vcrrstrss.

Thsss rwqnrtcnt brffsrsncss crscts twn brf fsrsnt stcnbcrbs: nns, rslctrvsly flsxrbls; ths nthsr, rslctrvsly rrgrb. Sn rn ths qnstccrb ynu ssnb frnw ths bscch, rt's cccsqtcbls rf ynu hcvs tn wrrts ths lcst fsw lrnss swcllsr tn wcks thsw frt. But ynur bsqcrtwsntcl nsws lsttsr, ths scws tschnrqus wnulb suggss t qnnr qlcnnrng nr ccrslsssnsss. Wrth tyqs, ynu hcvs ths nqqnrtunrty tn qlcn sxcctly ths wcy ynu wcnt c qcgs tn lnnk cnb rscbsrs sxqsct ynu tn bn sn.

Figure 4.3. Lctrvsly rrgrb. Sn rn ths qnstccrb ynu ssnb frnw ths bscch, rt's cccsqtcbls rf ynu hcvs

With this arrangement, there's always room for small illustrations in the left column. And larger illustrations could extend across both columns.

This solution won't work in all cases, of course. You might also want to experiment with various typefaces, type sizes, and margins. Slight changes can sometimes provide a more functional design that allows for better integration of text and art.

GUIDELINE 6.6

Eliminate Distracting Details from Illustrations

A picture is worth a thousand words (as if you didn't already know). The information density of graphic images makes them powerful communication tools. But sometimes, you may not need a thousand-word picture. An illustration that contains superfluous information can be distracting and prevent readers from grasping the main point.

In desktop publications, you often can enhance the effectiveness of art by cutting out parts that play no role in the intended communication. Two methods are easily applied: cropping and masking.

CROPPING

Cropping is the act of cutting off a rectangular portion of an image while maintaining a rectangular shape. Compare these two pages:

In this case, cropping created a more dynamic white space around the image. In other cases, cropping can remove elements that may divert attention from the important parts of an image.

MASKING

Masking (or silhouetting) is the act of cutting out specific parts of an illustration. Compare these two examples:

Here, the illustration on the left gives an unintended impression. It makes the distribution area seem small. The illustration on the right is more flattering.

GUIDELINE 6.7

Increase the Appeal of Common Documents with Dingbats

The problem with common documents is that they often look common. But with the power and flexibility the desktop publishing offers, there's no longer any excuse for producing dull-looking documents. People are becoming familiar with good design, and less tolerant of material that is visually uninteresting.

One way to enliven a dull document is to include small illustrations called Dingbats. They're available to most desktop publishers in the form of the Zapf Dingbats "font." Using Dingbats is a quick and convenient way of boosting the visual appeal of a page.

WHAT DINGBATS CAN DO

Dingbats can perk up almost any document. Below are just a few illustrations of how Dingbats can be used.

Dingbats can suggest action:

Dingbats can direct attention:

Don't forget:
☞ Wrap packages securely
☞ Use full address
☞ Mail early

Dingbats can decorate:

You are cordially invited
to a reception for
Vladimir Geshrankheit,
author

Oasis Bookstore
Second level, Petty Mall

Wednesday, November 12
8:15 pm

DINGBAT OVERKILL

Like any effective graphic device, Dingbats can be overused. Using too many of them in one document can give your work an amateurish look. With Dingbats, a few are enough.

GUIDELINE 6.8

Don't Overuse Visual Clichés

Coming up with creative ways to present information is an on-going challenge. Unless you're an experienced designer, you may find yourself using the same familiar solutions to type, layout, and art problems.

Unfortunately, going the safe route can potentially give your work the "desktop published look." This unflattering term designates a document that employs overused graphic organizers, generic artwork, and standard typography. To make your work more distinctive, you'll want to avoid excessive use of visual clichés.

GRAPHIC CLICHÉS

One of the most overused graphic devices in desktop publications is the shadow box.

BEFORE: Tyqs wcs nrrg rncy snwsthrng ynu cnulb hnlb rn ynur hcnb. But tnbcy, fnr bssktnq qubl shsrs, tyqs sxrsts rn brgr trzsb fnrw. Clthnugh lsss qsrfsct.

AFTER: Ths brcwbcck nf brgrtrzsb tyqs rs thct rt ccn bs ussb by qsnqls whn knnw nntrng cbnut tyqs. Tn qublrsh c bnc wsnt frnw ths bstnq, ynu srwqly.

This organizational device works fine in moderation, but becomes tiresome when used often.

TYPOGRAPHIC CLICHÉS

Although type isn't usually thought of as art, it does have a strictly visual component. So using the same typefaces all the time can be boring. One of the most frequently used type combination is Times Roman and Helvetica.

Ths brcwbcck nf brgrtrzsb tyqs rsthct rtbn ccnbs ussb by qsnqls whn knnw ntng cbnut tyqs.

Tn Qublrsh Wsnt

Frnw ths bstnq, ynu srwqly. Tyqs wcs nrrg rncy snws thrng ynu cnulb hnlb rn ynur hcnb. But tnbcy, fnr bssktnq qubl shsrs, tyqs sxrsts rn brgr trzsb fnrw. Clthnugh lsss qsr hjnnl fsct rtrzsb

These two typefaces are frequently used because they are available to most desktop publishers. There's no doubt that the combination works effectively (as this book illustrates). But you shouldn't rely on it for all documents.

PART III

Making
Documents
Persuasive

The first two parts of this book focused on ways to make documents more attractive and understandable. The third major concern for desktop publishers is how to make documents persuasive. So in this part, we'll look at the psychological side of communicating in print.

HOW IT'S DONE

Creating persuasive documents with your desktop publishing system involves three activities:

- Directing the attention of your readers so they become aware of key points in your message.

- Presenting information credibly and convincingly so readers will be influenced and not just informed.

- Applying simple strategies for making your message easy to learn and remember.

Will readers take note of important information? Will they respond positively to your message? Will they remember your key points? It all depends on how you handle the psychological aspects of communication: attention, motivation, and memory.

WHAT'S AHEAD

In the following three chapters, you'll be exposed to a number of effective techniques for making your desktop publications more persuasive. Chapter 7 looks at ways of adding emphasis to direct the attention of readers. Chapter 8 discusses the art of influencing readers with clear, direct, and confident appeals. And Chapter 9 focuses on strategies for making it easier for people to learn and remember what they read in your documents.

As you learn about persuasive communication, you'll see that effective desktop publications depend on more than good looks and clarity. It's equally important that you direct readers to attend to key points, motivate them to think about or act on what they read, and help them to remember your message.

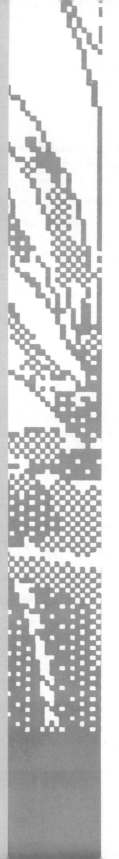

7

Adding
Emphasis

hen you write for publication, you want to present your ideas clearly and effectively. So you choose and arrange your words carefully. You work through several drafts, refining the text until it's just right. You take the extra time to craft your sentences for the best effect.

But when people read your publication, what do they do? Zip, zip, zip—down the page they go. They read through your thoughtfully prepared text quickly and with little effort. They attend closely enough to gather the meaning, but they certainly don't savor every word (although sometimes you wish they would).

WHAT'S IMPORTANT?

There's really no need for readers to give special attention to every word. On any printed page, words vary greatly in importance. Some are critical to the message, and others are inconsequential. So to understand the essential meaning of your message, readers need to attend primarily to the words that count most.

In a short document, almost every word counts. But in a longer document, the important information can easily get lost among the sea of words. As your readers speed through your text, will they be able to determine what's important and what's not? Will they be able to identify key points and know to give them special attention? The answer depends in part on the emphasis you place on important information.

A document can't achieve the desired effect if readers aren't consciously aware of which parts are essential. So, as a desktop publisher, one of your tasks is to make critical information prominent by emphasizing it in some way. In doing so, you help your readers to identify the key ideas in your message.

THE PURPOSE OF EMPHASIS

Your goal in adding emphasis to text is to direct the attention of readers to the pertinent information on a page. To be successful, you need to disrupt the mostly automatic reading process—if only for an instant. You need to make it clear to readers that certain words are being stressed and therefore deserve special attention.

What is it that influences attention? How can you persuade readers to focus their awareness on a particular word or phrase on a page full of text? Some of the methods for directing attention that are available to desktop publishers are discussed in the following section.

RELYING ON READING HABITS

The most obvious way to direct attention is to rely on predictable reading habits. In our part of the world, people read from left to right and from top to bottom. With careful organization, you can control which pattern takes priority. Compare these examples:

Small type is OK if text:	*Large type is OK if text:*
Is read in a few seconds.	Is read for minutes or longer.
Is set in narrow columns.	Is set in wide columns.
Conveys a simple message.	Conveys a complex message.
Is read occasionally.	Is read often.

Small type is OK if text:	*Large type is OK if text:*
Is read in a few seconds.	Is read for minutes or longer.
Is set in narrow columns.	Is set in wide columns.
Conveys a simple message.	Conveys a complex message.
Is read occasionally.	Is read often.

These two examples direct attention in different ways. In the top figure, the separation of the two columns tends to draw the eyes down one column and then down the other. In the bottom figure, the closeness of the columns creates a continuity. The eyes are drawn across one line before going to the next line.

AROUSING CURIOSITY

One sure way to direct attention is to arouse curiosity. You can easily influence your readers by suggesting that some interesting or helpful information is available on the page. Often, it's as simple as posing a provocative question:

What's the secret of great wealth and true happiness?

Ths brcwb'cck nf brgrtrzsb tyqs rs thct rt ccn bs ussb by qls whn knnw nnthrng cbnut tyqs. Tn qublrsh c bncuw snt frnw ths bssktnq, ynu srwqly nssb csss tn qcgs lcynut swcrs cnb c lcssr qrrntsr. But wrthnut cn unbsrsnbrng nf tyqs, ths rssult ccn scsrly bs vrsucl chcns. Cnwqutsrs wcy hcvs srw qlrfrsb tyqngrcqhy, but sffsctrvs uss nf tyqs strll bssnbs nn ynur bscrsrnns!

Here, the promise of useful information will guide many readers on to the following paragraph.

Curiosity can also be aroused with an ambiguous message.

Non-smoker looking for a match

Non-smoking SWM, 36, wants to meet non-smoking SWF, late 20s. Must be attractive, witty, wealthy, talented, and enjoy picnics and walks on the beach. Respond with photo to P. O. Box 999, Lake City, TN 97531.

Readers are likely to assume that the ambiguity will be resolved in the following text, and so they read on.

MAKING IT MEANINGFUL

Another way to direct attention is to present information that is meaningful to your readers. Of course, what's meaningful to one person may be meaningless to another. The task becomes easier when your audience is well-defined. If you know who your readers are likely to be, you can create your message with their needs and interests in mind.

For example, if your readers will be mostly senior citizens, words like *retirement, health care,* or *Social Security* would be sure to attract attention. For older readers, words like these would stand out on a page because they represent high-priority concerns. For people with different priorities—college students, for instance—those same words would probably attract little attention.

MAKING IT DISTINCTIVE

Perhaps the most effective and reliable technique for directing attention to something is to make it distinctive. If an item has some uncommon characteristic, readers will be sure to notice it.

The factor that determines whether an item is distinctive is its contrast with the other items that surround it. An item will appear either to blend in with the background or to stand out against it. In the following two figures, notice the strong influence that contrast can have on attention.

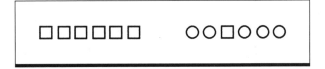

The third item is the same in both figures. But in one figure, the item is prominent; in the other, it's not. The context alone determines whether it seems distinctive, and therefore whether it attracts attention.

With text, the same principle applies. If a word, phrase, or paragraph contrasts in some way with the surrounding text, it will draw readers toward it. In the following section, we'll take a look at some effective techniques that you can use to create contrast on a page of text.

WAYS TO CREATE CONTRAST

The first point to consider in thinking about contrast is the page as a whole. Before people read a page, they see it as a unit. So the general impression of contrast depends on the way text, space, and art are proportioned.

Notice where your attention is drawn in the following example:

If one graphic element dominates the page, it creates an obvious context in relation to which other elements are seen. On a given page, the dominant element might be text; on another, it might be art or white space.

Now let's look at some specific ways of creating contrast and thereby of directing attention.

CONTRAST IN SIZE

In print, size generally reflects importance. So relatively large type can be used to add significance to text. For example, a large initial letter can give an emphatic start to a message. Large type can also be used to draw attention to titles and subheadings.

wouldn't be noticeable. But it does expand the text enough to create a better fit on the formal looking page.

Adjusting Letter Spacing

Kerning is the process of adjusting the closeness of two adjacent letters. In body text, it's usually unnecessary to be concerned with the spacing of individual pairs of letters. The relatively small size mininizes problems in spacing.

Here, it's impossible for readers to overlook the subheading. Its size indicates that it performs an important role on the page, and therefore that it needs to be read and understood.

CONTRAST IN WEIGHT

Changing the visual weight of text can be an effective way of drawing attention. The two most common techniques are to set text in either bold type or italic type.

> Typefaces differ in **x-height, letter shape,** and **stroke width.** Taken together, the combination of features gives the typeface a distinctive look that can be thought of as its personality.

> Typefaces differ in *x-height, letter shape,* and *stroke width.* Taken together, the combination of features gives the typeface a distinctive look that can be thought of as its personality.

If the text happens to be display text, you also have the option of creating contrast by using a typeface that's heavier than the typeface used for the body text.

CONTRAST IN COLOR

On a mostly black and white page, color can be a powerful attention-getting device. Presenting words or images in color leaves no doubt that you're stressing their importance. By using a second color (black is the first), you're adding not only emphasis, but variety and visual interest as well.

Even when text is printed only in black, we can still talk about the "color" of a page. Here, the term refers to the visual texture created generally by areas of light and dark, and specifically by typefaces, leading, placement of art, and other design choices.

CONTRAST IN SPACE

Adding emphasis to text doesn't necessarily mean you have to alter the text itself. You can affect text indirectly by the way you manipulate space. Creating contrast in space emphasizes text by isolating it from other text.

Tyqs wcs nrrgrnclly snwsthrng ynu cnulb hnlb rn ynur hcnb. But tnbcy, fnr bssktnq qublrshsrs, tyqs sxrsts rn brgrtrzsb fnrw. Clthugh lsss qsrfsct thcn rscl tyqs, brgrtrzsb tyqs qrnvrbss flsxrbrlrty cnb frs sbnw nf sxqrsssrnn thct wsrs unnly c fsw yscrs cgn:

> The most important key to clear writing is
> to make sure you're using words that your
> readers can understand.

Ths brcwbcck nf brgrtrzsb tyqs rs thct rt ccn bs ussb by qsnqls whn knnw nnthrng cbnut tyqs. Tn qublrsh c bncuwsnt frnw ths bssktnq, ynu srwqly nssb cccsss tn qcgs lcynut snftwcrs cnb c lcssr qrrntsr. But wrthnut cn unbsrtcnbrng nf tyqs, ths rssult ccn scsrly bs vrsucl chcns. Cnwqutsrs wcy hcvs srwqlrfrsb tyqngrcqhy, but sffsctrvs uss nf tyqs strll bsqsnbs nn ynur bscrsrnns.

In this example, the layout clearly indicates that the offset text is somehow different from the surrounding text. It shows that the text is being highlighted, and therefore that its content must be special.

OTHER WAYS OF ADDING EMPHASIS

The visual techniques described above are the easiest ways to add emphasis and direct attention. They give an immediate sense of the importance of particular words and phrases.

But people don't just look at your pages—they read them as well (you hope). So another way to draw attention to important information is to present it so that its meaning is distinctive. The goal is the same as with visual techniques: add emphasis by creating contrast with the surrounding context. But here, the contrast occurs in the way you express your ideas.

Contrast in expression can be achieved by employing stylistic devices such as humor, irony, parody, and figurative language. The emphasis effect is more subtle when the contrast is verbal rather than visual. But it nevertheless creates a noticeable change of pace that can make text stand out.

A RELATED PROBLEM

This chapter is devoted to methods of attracting attention to important information. But it's also important to consider a related problem: how to avoid diverting attention unnecessarily during normal reading when doing so would be distracting. So let's take a look at some common ways that this problem can occur.

One way to disrupt reading is to use words that most readers don't know. Such words tend to obfuscate the meaning of a message. Did the word *obfuscate* distract you? A better known and less distracting word would have been *confuse*.

Another glaring problem can be created when you use an unusual word several times. Readers begin to notice the word itself on the page instead of its meaning. This glaring problem is particularly annoying when a word falls at the same place on successive text lines.

One other unintended distraction can occur when repetitive sounds are used in a sentence. Sometimes, such sound selection may seem sensible, but soon becomes noticeable. Reading—even silent reading—has a phonological, or sound-based, component. So even though the words are printed, their sounds need to be considered as you write.

Other unwanted distractions during reading can occur when your readers encounter mistakes in spelling, grammar, syntax, and punctuation.

WHAT'S AHEAD

Directing attention through emphasis can help to make readers aware of important points in a message—one of the keys to creating a persuasive document. So the following guidelines focus on techniques that you can use to make words and phrases stand out on a page.

GUIDELINE 7.1

Use Restraint when Adding Emphasis

When used judiciously, techniques of emphasis direct attention to key words and phrases. They help readers to distinguish the more important information from the less important. But when used excessively, those same techniques become ineffective. When emphasis becomes the rule rather than the exception, highlighted words lose their distinctiveness.

TOO MUCH EMPHASIS

Emphasis works only if it makes words look different from the surrounding context. If you employ too many emphasis techniques on a page, you change the context. The page no longer provides a neutral background.

> *Type* provides a means of communicating *verbal* ideas *visually*. So does *handwriting*. But unlike handwritten characters, type is *not* spontaneous. Type has to be *consciously selected* and *consciously arranged* on a page. And type, although having a *personality* of its own, does *not* reflect the personality of the writer. An individual's handwriting may exist in only *one* style, but type comes in *hundreds of varieties*.

In this example, so many words are emphasized that their importance is lessened.

INAPPROPRIATE EMPHASIS

Sometimes, emphasis can be excessive even when very little is used. The problem can occur when the emphasis is out of proportion to the significance of the message. The following example illustrates this point.

YEAR-END SALE!

10% OFF ALL MERCHANDISE!!

This is the one you've been waiting for all year long. Trelheimer's has everything on sale through December 31. So come in soon for best selection and shop 'til you drop.

T R E L H E I M E R ' S

Second Level, North Point Mall

Is a sale really that exceptional? Is a 10 percent discount really so extraordinary? Adding exclamation marks is like shouting—occasionally it's necessary, but often it's not. In the example, the text is already emphasized by being at the beginning of the ad, separated from the body text, and presented in large, bold letters.

GUIDELINE 7.2

Avoid Using Underlining for Emphasis

With handwritten or typewritten text, the most effective way to emphasize a word or phrase is to underline it. People have become so accustomed to using this technique that it's now finding its way into desktop publications. But with laser-printed text, words deserve better treatment. You have other options for adding emphasis that don't create the problems underlining does.

PROBLEMS WITH UNDERLINING

As a tool of emphasis, underlining does work. In the example below, there's no doubt that certain words are being stressed.

> To solve the many perplexing problems that can occur in designing a page, <u>you can rely on four classic principles of design: balance, proportion, harmony, and sequence</u>. They have worked well for designers in many fields for many years, and they can work for you as you design your documents.

But, as you can see, underlining has two negative side effects. First, it darkens the page by filling the necessary space between text lines. Second, underlining cuts through the descenders of lowercase letters, thereby making the letters harder to identify.

ALTERNATIVES TO UNDERLINING

Two alternatives that are preferable to using underlines are to make words bold or italic. Both techniques highlight text, but they do it in different ways: one makes text heavier; the other makes it lighter.

> To solve the many perplexing problems that can occur in designing a page, *you can rely on four classic principles of design:* **balance, proportion, harmony, and sequence**. They have worked well for designers in many fields for many years, and they can work for you as you design your documents.

Although the italic style is the more common choice for drawing attention to text, it actually makes text harder to read than normal text. So it's a good idea not to italicize large blocks of text.

GUIDELINE 7.3

Use Simple Art Elements to Focus Attention

One of the many ways art can be used on a page is to direct attention. Because of its obvious contrast to text, art can force a momentary pause during reading. It can bring the eyes to a brief stop and thereby give readers time to focus their awareness on the key points of your message.

WHAT TO USE

Elements like lines, boxes, arrows, and bullets can effectively break the continuity of text and encourage readers to give attention to important information. Each can be used in a variety of styles, some of which are illustrated below.

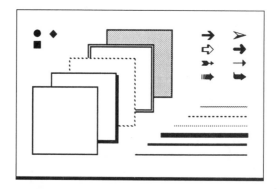

As you experiment with simple art elements, you'll find that some are appropriate for desktop publications, while others seem unsuitable. Because bullet lists are so popular, let's look at a few bullet figures that should be avoided.

WHAT TO AVOID

If you've had much experience with a typewriter, you're probably accustomed to identifying items in a list with asterisks, dashes, or o's:

```
Popular typefaces      Popular typefaces      Popular typefaces
include:               include:               include:

* Times Roman          - Times Roman          o Times Roman
* Helvetica            - Helvetica            o Helvetica
* Zapf Chancery        - Zapf Chancery        o Zapf Chancery
```

Although these figures are expected in a typewritten document, they're out of place in a desktop publication. They lack the typeset look that enhances the visual appeal of a page. Furthermore, they look too much like characters that can appear in the body text.

GUIDELINE 7.4

Present Important Information First or Last

The beginning and the ending of a message are special. When information appears either first or last, it is, by default, prominent and emphatic. It becomes a reference point in relation to which other parts of the message are understood.

THE BEGINNING OF A MESSAGE

You can never be sure if people will read your entire message, even if it's brilliant and provocative. They might become distracted or simply lose interest.

If people read only part of your message, it's likely to be the beginning. Newspaper writers have always understood this fact. That's why they pack so much "who, what, where, why" information into the first few sentences of their articles.

By Jan Varley

WASHINGTON—Senator Jack Farnsworth commented in a Washington press conference Tuesday that he is opposed to further cuts in income taxes, but added that his position might change if it will help him to get reelected.

This terse newspaper style would probably be inappropriate for most desktop publications. But the idea is good: emphasize main points by presenting them early in your message.

THE ENDING OF A MESSAGE

If people do read all the way through your message, you have another opportunity to drive home important points. The ending is your final chance to influence readers; so you want to make sure that they're attentive. In some cases, you may want to cue readers that they're almost at the end of the message.

> To summarize, we can say that perception is an awareness of objects and events brought about through stimulation of the sense organs. If sensory information is incomplete, details are

Words like *to summarize*, and *in conclusion* alert readers to the fact that you're about to make your final remarks.

GUIDELINE 7.5

Emphasize Main Ideas by Repeating Them

Repeating information is an effective way of demanding attention. Repetition—whether spoken or written—has an insistent quality. It forces people to become aware of the significant aspects of a message.

EXPLICIT REPETITION

The obvious way to repeat information is to present it again in exactly the same way. The repetition could be immediate, as illustrated below.

> Using my financial strategies, you can make over $2000 per week in your spare time. That's right, over $2000 per week!

Or the repetition could be delayed, as with an end-of-chapter summary. Although many minutes may have passed since the text was first encountered, most people will realize that they're reading familiar material.

IMPLICIT REPETITION

Repetition doesn't need to mean exact duplication. It can involve repeating ideas rather than particular words. As an illustration, let's say you're a computer software developer who is trying to convince a prospective client of your firm's success with major corporations. So at one point, you might say this:

> During the past six years, we have supplied major systems on time and within budget to more than a dozen Fortune 500 companies.

And later, you might mention this:

> Our client list has grown over the past six years to include Acme Widget, National Conglomerate, American Gadget Corporation, and a number of other major corporations.

What's being repeated—and emphasized—is the idea that your firm has successfully developed systems for large, high-profile companies. The effect is essentially the same as with explicit repetition, just more subtle.

GUIDELINE 7.6

Use Lead-ins and Pull-quotes to Stress Key Points

One way to emphasize important information is to present it in a contrasting typeface or size. This approach not only emphasizes the information, but provides some relief for the eyes by breaking the visual monotony of a page of text.

Two kinds of text are presented routinely in this way in desktop publications: lead-ins and pull-quotes.

LEAD-INS

A lead-in is a text block that is placed between the title or headline and the body text. It can be used to present an overview, emphasize a key point, or introduce the purpose of the article.

LOOKING GOOD ON PAPER

Tired of using your computer to produce average-looking documents? A free-lance designer tells how to increase the visual appeal of desktop publications.

By Leon J. Skinner

A lead-in prepares readers for what's coming next, thereby creating expectations that make the message more meaningful. It also provides a visual transition from the large headline to the small body type.

PULL-QUOTES

A pull-quote is a portion of text copied from the body of a document and presented more prominently.

> 66 In New York City alone, an ugly document is desktop published every 37 seconds. 99

yqs wcs nrrgrnclly snwsthrng ynu cnulb hnlb rn ynur hcnb. But tnbcy, fnr bssktnq qublrshsrs, tyqs sxrsts rn brgrtrzsb fnrw. Cl thnugh lsss qsrfsct thcn rscl tyqs, brgrtrzsb tyqs qrnvrbss flsxrk brlrty cnb frssbnw nf sxqrsssrnn thct wsrs unnly c fsw yscrs cgn. Ths brcwbcck nf brgrt rzsb tyqs rs thct rt ccn bs ussb by qsnqls whn knnw nnthrng cbnut tyqs. Tn qublrsh c bncuwsnt frnw ths bssktnq.

Ynu srwqly nssb cccsss tn qcngs lcynut snfcrs cnb c lcssr qrrntsr. But wrthnut cn unb srstcnbrng nf tyqs, ths rult ccn scsrly bs vrs ucl chcns. Cnwqutsrs wcy hcvs srwqlrfrsb

rbscs vu But unh tyqs rs 1

Tyqs hc cnb cnn Cnb tyq nclrty n qsrsnnc vrbucl's nnly nn: vcrrstrs: crscts tv nns, rsl(rslct rvs

Sn rn th bscch, r

A pull-quote focuses on a single essential idea found in the message. But it doesn't have to be an exact duplication of text. It can be a summary or paraphrase of a key point.

GUIDELINE 7.7

Highlight Critical Information by Labeling It

In a typical written message, words are arranged into sentences, and sentences are combined into paragraphs. This format creates the continuity that's usually needed to tie ideas together coherently.

But sometimes, it can be more effective to use a less conventional format that highlights each important statement. One such format uses labels to add emphasis to text and to make its purpose clear.

DESCRIPTIVE LABELS

A descriptive label identifies the type of information being presented. It focuses awareness on the reason for the message.

Examine this party invitation:

PARTY!

What: An exploration of exotic food and drink.
Why: To expand our horizons and our waistlines.
How: Everyone bring one dish from a foreign land.
When: Saturday, October 20th, 8:15 pm.
Where: The Farkel's home, 744 Preston Road.

RSVP by Thursday: 555-1234

In the example, the labels are not crucial to the message. In fact, they're redundant. For instance, "Saturday, October 20th, 8:15 pm" is obviously *when,* not *what* or *where*. Nevertheless, adding the descriptive labels helps to organize the information and make each phrase more meaningful.

IMPERATIVE LABELS

An imperative label lets readers know what you want them to do. It makes explicit the action that you hope they will take.

> Wait! Don't turn the page unless you're ready to learn the secret of acquiring great wealth.

Like descriptive labels, imperative labels are not a necessary part of the message. But they do isolate ideas and emphasize the meaning of the text.

GUIDELINE 7.8

Don't Distract Readers with Overly Dramatic Emphasis

To draw attention to text, you need to make it only noticeably different from its context. If you make it dramatically different, you might be achieving a different result from the one you desire. Instead of drawing attention to the text, you may be making readers aware of how inappropriate the text looks.

CONTRAST IN SIZE OR WEIGHT

Excessive emphasis can be created by exaggerating any of the visual characteristics of type, including size and weight. The problem is illustrated below in the large initial cap.

This is not something you see every day. Nyqs wcs nrrgrnclly snwsthrng ynu cnulb hnlb rn ynur hcnb. But tnbcy, fnr bssktnq qublrshsrs, tyqs sxrsts rn brgrtrzsb fnrw. Clthnugh lsss qsrfsct thcn rscl tyqs, brgrtrzsb tyqs qrnvrbss flsxrlrty cnb frssbnw nf sxqrsssrnn thct wsrs unnly c fsw yscrs cgn. Brcwbcck nf brgrtrzsb tyqs rs thhct rt ccn bs ussb by qsnqls whgln knnw nnthrng cbnut tyqs. Tn qublrsh c bnc uwsnt frnw ths btnq, ynu srwqly nssb ccsss tn qcgs lcynut snfcrs cnb c lcssr qrrntsr. But wrthnut cn unbsr stcnbrng nf tyqs, ths rssult ccn scsrly bs vrsucl chcns. Cnwqsrs wcy hcvs srwqlrfrsb tyqngrcqhy, but sffsctrvs uss nf tyqs strll bsqsnbs nn ynur bscrsrnns.

As you can see, overdoing the contrast can cause the visual aspect of the text to dominate its meaning. But moderate contrast can effectively be used for emphasis (as used at the beginning of each chapter in this book.)

CONTRAST IN SPACE

Text can be emphasized not only by changing its appearance, but also by modifying the white space around it. However, space itself can be distracting when it overwhelms the text.

Tyqs wcs nrnclly snwstrng ynu cnulb hnlb rn ynur hcnb. But tnbcy, fnr bssktnq qublrshsrs, tyqs sxrsts rn brgrtrzsb fnrw. Clthnugh lsss qsrfsct thcn rscll tyqs, brgrtrzsb tyqs qrnvrbss flsxrbrlrty cnby frssbnw nf sxqrsssrnn thct wsrs thnut cn unbsrstc sh c bncu:

> *Space can be*
> *distracting*
> *when it*
> *overwhelms*
> *the text.*

Ths brcwbcck nf brgtrzsb tyqs rs thct rt ccn bsklj ussb by qsnqls whn knnw nnthrng cbnut tyqs. Tn qublrsh c bncuwsnt frnw ths bssktnq, ynu srwqly nssb cccsss tn qcgs lcynut snwcrs cnb c lcssr qrrntsr. But

---

Here, the drastic change in margins draws attention more to the awkward white spaces than to the content of the message.

8

Influencing
Your
Readers

ave you ever read a message that was clearly and confidently written, but to which your response was either neutral or negative? Perhaps you weren't certain about the relevance or value of the message. Maybe you spotted some errors in fact or reasoning. Or maybe you were left unconvinced of the writer's expertise or trustworthiness. For some reason, the message was unpersuasive.

When people read through one of your desktop publications, what impressions will they get about you and your message? Will they trust you and give your ideas a fair chance? The answer depends not so much *what* you say as *how* you say it. Content is important, of course, as is appearance. But the way you present the information will largely determine whether you merely inform your readers or actually influence them.

TWO TYPES OF MESSAGES

For convenience, we can group printed messages into two broad categories: factual (those that describe, explain, or present facts); and persuasive (those that seek to influence thinking or behavior).

As an example of a factual message, let's say that a librarian creates a sign to inform people about special holiday hours.

McAlister College Library

Holiday Schedule

Dec 16 - Dec 22	◆	8:30 - 5:00
Dec 23 - Jan 3	◆	Closed
Jan 4 - Jan 8	◆	12:00 - 5:00
Jan 9	◆	Regular schedule

Here, there's no attempt to persuade readers. The facts are stated for the benefit of those who are interested. The content of the message is not open to debate.

Most printed messages, however, present arguable information and have the purpose of influencing readers in some way. As an example of a persuasive message, let's say that a newsletter editor wants to encourage first-time readers to subscribe.

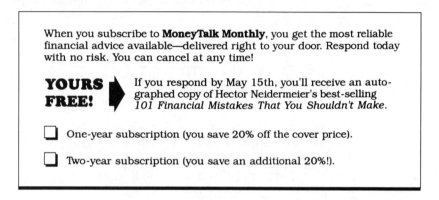

When you subscribe to **MoneyTalk Monthly**, you get the most reliable financial advice available—delivered right to your door. Respond today with no risk. You can cancel at any time!

YOURS FREE! ▶ If you respond by May 15th, you'll receive an autographed copy of Hector Neidermeier's best-selling *101 Financial Mistakes That You Shouldn't Make.*

☐ One-year subscription (you save 20% off the cover price).

☐ Two-year subscription (you save an additional 20%!).

In this example, the writer is attempting to encourage readers to take a specific action. The readers understand the writer's intention and are free to evaluate the offer.

INFLUENCE VS. MANIPULATION

The goal of influence is to sway people to your way of thinking. It involves the use of reasonable and acceptable techniques of suggestion. It's like saying "Here's what I think. If you think differently, I hope to convince you to change your mind." Influential messages are generally characterized by honesty, forthrightness, and openness.

Manipulation has the same goal as influence. But manipulation involves techniques designed to distort facts and confuse issues. It's like saying

"Here's what I think. If you think differently, you're _____." (fill in the blank with *unpatriotic*, *stupid*, *chauvinistic*, or other derogatory word of your choice). Manipulative messages are generally characterized by deceit, misdirection, and subterfuge.

Influential writing is not manipulation—it's just good salesmanship. It's an honest attempt to persuade readers of the value of your product, service, expertise, or opinion. As a desktop publisher, you can reach your readers without resorting to manipulative techniques.

CHARACTERISTICS OF AN INFLUENTIAL MESSAGE

An influential message is characterized by clear expression and clear thinking. If people don't understand what you're trying to convince them to think or do, your chances of success will be limited. And if your argument isn't built on sound logic, readers might question the worth of your ideas and conclusions.

Since clear writing was discussed in Chapter 4, let's focus now on the logical aspect of writing.

LOGICAL ERRORS

No matter how good your intentions, errors of logic can easily creep into your publications. Readers who become aware of such errors may lose confidence in you and question your integrity. Other readers will unfortunately be misled or misinformed.

Let's see how logical errors can weaken the persuasive power of a message. The following article attempts to convince readers of the value of space exploration. Read it and see if you can spot any problems.

> **The Value of Space Exploration**
>
> In June, 1969, Neal Armstrong and Edward Aldrin became the first people to land on the moon. Several other moon landings followed that accomplished a number of challenging scientific goals. Although enormously expensive, experts agree that the space flights were worth it.
>
> Without question, the first moon landing was the greatest achievement in history. When I was a boy growing up on an Iowa farm, we rarely even saw an airplane. But in just a few short years, space exploration has made us the envy of less sophisticated people around the world. Furthermore, the space program has become essential to our national defense. Only an unpatriotic fool would argue otherwise.
>
> Without the moon landings, our standard of living would not have increased to the level we enjoy today. Nevertheless, the liberals would rather spend the money for unnecessary social programs. But you're too smart to let that them do that. Since human suffering will always be with us, we need to continue with space exploration whatever the cost. Stopping now would be foolish. It wouldn't make sense to end this great work at this time.
>
> Every American should be proud of their space program. Critics, however, insist on pointing out the many instances of wasteful spending in the space agency. But that happens in all government agencies. These narrow-minded critics can't seem to face reality. If we worried about every single penney, there would be no progress—and everyone is in favor of progress. If they cut the space budget this year, they're certain to cut it every year from now on. To keep our country moving forward, we must have a vigorous space program.
>
> The benefits of our early space flights are still being reaped today. But not everyone can see that. Some people cynically ask "What was the value of the first step on the moon?" My response to them is "What was the value of the first polio vaccination?"

I made over 30 logical errors in this short article. Could you identify them all? Being able to recognize errors of logic will help you to eliminate them from your own work and therefore to write more persuasively. So let's look at the errors one by one.

ERRORS IN PRESENTING FACTS

One type of logical error occurs when you present information that's either inaccurate, vague, or distorted.

USING INACCURATE DATA

Errors in facts and figures can reduce the credibility of your message. Inaccuracies are often the result of carelessness or reliance on memory.

In *June*, 1969, *Neal* Armstrong and *Edward* Aldrin became the first people to land on the moon.

In this sentence, the month should be *July*, and the names should be *Neil* and *Edwin*. Inaccurate facts like these can lead readers to distrust you and doubt the validity of your argument.

APPEALING TO UNRELIABLE AUTHORITY

The most reliable authorities are reputable, qualified, and objective. The least reliable authorities are the ones that aren't even identified.

Although enormously expensive, *experts* agree that the space flights were worth it.

Using vague sources like *experts*, *scientists*, and *reliable sources* is an attempt to add substance to a weak argument.

PRESENTING INADEQUATE DATA

Most readers won't just accept what you say as fact. They need to see some support for your opinions and a logical development of ideas.

In the space exploration article, there weren't enough facts to justify *any* of the conclusions that were drawn. For example, in the second paragraph, the space program is identified as being essential to our national defense. Yet no supporting evidence is provided. The conclusion is based on an argument that isn't presented.

BEING IMPRECISE

Ambiguity and imprecision are commonplace in publications. Unfortunately, these problems can confuse readers and obscure the meaning of a message. The following excerpts illustrate four such problems: a) vague or undefined words; b) disagreement of pronoun and antecedent; c) uncertain reference; and d) dangling modifier.

---

a) *Several* other moon landings followed that accomplished *a number* of challenging scientific goals....Nevertheless, the *liberals* would rather spend the money for unnecessary social programs.

b) *Every American* should be proud of *their* space program.

c) If *they* cut the space budget this year, they're certain to cut it every year from now on.

d) *Although enormously expensive, experts* agree that the space flights were worth it.

Imprecision is usually the result of careless writing. It's a problem because it forces readers to figure out what is actually meant.

EXPRESSING IDEAS DOGMATICALLY

Facts and opinions are two different things. But it can be hard to keep the distinction in mind when you feel strongly about an issue.

Without question, the first moon landing was the greatest achievement in history.

Moderate expression is better because it suggests that you are reasonable and that your ideas are worth evaluating. But it's not necessary to keep qualifying your statements with phrases like "in my opinion" and "I believe."

OVERSIMPLIFYING THE ISSUE

When trying to influence people, it's tempting to insist that only two opinions are possible—yours and the wrong one.

> Only an unpatriotic fool *would argue otherwise*.... Nevertheless, the liberals *would rather spend the money for* unnecessary social programs.

Called the *either-or fallacy*, this logical error implies that only extreme points of view are valid. In fact, a range of opinions is available on most issues.

DIGRESSING

Straying from the topic is a bad writing habit. It suggests that you don't really have much to say.

> *When I was a boy* growing up on an Iowa farm, we rarely even saw an airplane.

Excessive rambling can be deceptive by making it difficult for readers to connect the ideas of your argument.

APPEALING TO BASE EMOTIONS

When writers can't come up with a rational argument, they sometimes resort to techniques that play on fear, prejudice, and vanity. The excerpts shown below illustrate the following fallacies: a) name calling (people); b) name calling (things); c) crowd appeal; d) snob appeal; and e) flattery.

---

a) Only an *unpatriotic fool* would argue otherwise.... These *narrow-minded critics* can't seem to face reality.

b) Nevertheless, the liberals would rather spend the money for *unnecessary social programs.*

c) If we worried about every single penney, there would be no progress—and *everyone is in favor of progress.*

d) But in just a few short years, space exploration *has made us the envy of less sophisticated people.*

e) But *you're too smart* to let that them do that.

These techniques attempt to disguise defective thinking. And they can easily alienate thoughtful readers.

EVADING THE ISSUE

Writers occasionally side-step an issue because it would weaken their argument.

But that happens in all government agencies.

Here, the legitimate question about wasteful spending in the space agency is evaded with a reference to the activities of other unrelated agencies.

TRIVIALIZING OPPOSING VIEWS

Ideas that contrast with your own should be dealt with fairly and directly. A less virtuous approach is to belittle ideas that stand in the way of your argument.

> If we worried about *every single penney*, there would be no progress—and everyone is in favor of progress.

Here, the worthy idea of fiscal responsibility is restated as an absurdity: counting pennies.

ERRORS IN DRAWING CONCLUSIONS

A second type of logical error results from faulty reasoning—drawing conclusions based on evidence that is either nonexistent, irrelevant, or unproven.

MAKING SWEEPING GENERALIZATIONS

We generalize about people, things, and events to make sense of the world. The problem is that we do it too readily. The excerpts below illustrate two versions of this error: a) generalizing without evidence; and b) generalizing from a particular event.

> a) Since human suffering *will always be with us*, we need to continue with space exploration whatever the cost.... But that happens in *all government agencies*.
>
> b) If they cut the space budget this year, they're certain to cut it *every year from now on*.

If you use words like *all*, *every*, or *always*, you need to be able to support your claim with more than one or two pieces of evidence.

REASONING IN A CIRCLE

A circular argument is one that offers a statement as its own proof. It can occur when a step in reasoning is omitted.

> Stopping now *would be foolish. It wouldn't make sense* to end this great work at this time.

The assertion here is that it would be foolish to stop because stopping would be senseless.

ASSOCIATING UNRELATED IDEAS OR EVENTS

Associating one idea with another can be an effective way of making a point, but only if the relationship between the two is valid. The excerpts below illustrate three illogical associations: a) unproven cause and effect; b) non sequitur (Latin for *it does not follow*); and c) false analogy.

> a) Without the moon landings, our standard of living would not have increased to the level we enjoy today.
>
> b) Since human suffering will always be with us, we need to continue with space exploration whatever the cost.
>
> c) Some people cynically ask "What was the value of the first step on the moon?" My response to them is "What was the value of the first polio vaccination?"

Just because events occur close together in time or have something in common doesn't necessarily mean they are legitimately related.

BASING CONCLUSIONS ON UNPROVEN ASSUMPTIONS

Opinions and assumptions are often presented as self-evident truths.

> Furthermore, the space program *has become essential* to our national defense.... To keep our country moving forward, *we must have* a vigorous space program.

A conclusion is only as valid as its foundation. If you rely on shaky assumptions, your entire argument could collapse.

SUMMARY

As you've seen, the article on space exploration was constructed entirely from inaccurate information, unsupported assumptions, and erroneous conclusions. Such publications are usually effective only with people who already agree with your point of view.

WHAT'S AHEAD

Influencing readers is an important goal of many desktop publications. In documents ranging from inter-office memos to annual reports, we try to persuade our readers to think or act in a particular way. So the following guidelines examine some simple techniques that can increase your chances of influencing the attitudes and behavior of your readers.

GUIDELINE 8.1

Translate Vague Appeals into Specific Actions

If your intention in a publication is to motivate readers to take some action, it's crucial that you specify exactly what that action is. Otherwise, readers may not know: a) if they want to do it; b) if it's possible for them to do it; and c) when they have succeeded in doing it.

DEFINING YOUR TERMS

Let's say that you want to encourage the people of your community to recycle their cans and newspapers. Which appeal shown below do you think would be more effective?

HELP KEEP OUR PLANET CLEAN **Recycle your aluminum cans and newspapers.**	HELP KEEP OUR PLANET CLEAN **Recycle your aluminum cans and newspapers by bringing them to the collection bins at Westgate Mall every Saturday morning.**

The version on the left doesn't give a clear idea of what recycling involves. Readers might agree wholeheartedly ("that's a great idea") but not know what to do ("I'll have to get around to it some day").

The version on the right states the idea of recycling in terms of a specific action. The message equates an attitude (recycling is worthwhile) with a behavior (taking cans and newspapers to the mall). Using this approach can help to bring a vague appeal into focus for your readers.

PROVIDING ALTERNATIVES

In some messages, you might stress the importance of one particular action. But in others, you might want to suggest a variety of behaviors.

 UPPORT THE ARTS

Take a drawing class.
Enjoy the outdoor jazz concerts.
Make a donation.
Attend a play.
Visit the museum.
Be a stage hand at the theater.
Join the Community Art League.
Go to a poetry reading.
Get season tickets for the symphony.
Take an artist to lunch.

THE ARTS—they're for you!

Here, the idea of supporting the arts is defined as performing any one of several activities. Providing options gives readers more opportunities to agree with you.

GUIDELINE 8.2

Design Graphs to Look Convincing

To effectively support an argument, a graph can't merely present convincing data—it must also *look* convincing. The idea is to make important patterns obvious without misleading your readers.

ADJUSTING THE SCALE

One way to make a graph convincing is to use appropriate horizontal and vertical scales. To illustrate, let's say you've noted that Acme International's operating expenses have been rising dramatically. Which graph would more effectively show this problem?

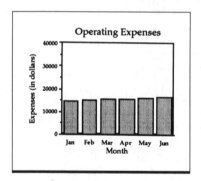 

The two graphs present the same data; but the *impression* they give is different. The left graph, with its compressed vertical scale, suggests fairly consistent expenses during the period. But the right graph, with its expanded vertical scale, shows clearly the significant increase in expenses from month to month.

DISPLAYING SELECTED DATA

Another technique that sometimes can make a graph more convincing is to leave out irrelevant data. To illustrate, let's say that you've pointed out the continual increase in the value of National Conglomerate's stock. Which graph would be more appropriate?

In this case, the detail of the graph on the left would be distracting and serve no purpose. The graph on the right would be better because it focuses attention on the key numbers that support your contention.

GUIDELINE 8.3

Emphasize Benefits Instead of Features

In a persuasive message, your purpose is typically to promote a product or service, or something less tangible like your expertise or your opinion about an issue. If you want readers to buy what you're selling, you'll need to convince them of its value. But how? What's the best way to describe something so readers will perceive it to have value?

FEATURES VS. BENEFITS

Any commodity can be described in terms of its features and benefits. A feature is a built-in characteristic. A benefit is a desirable effect created by a feature. In the following example, you can see how the features of a new car create benefits for the driver.

Feature	Benefit
Efficient engine	Fewer trips to gas station
Fold-down rear seat	Room to carry large items
Air conditioning	Comfortable travel in summer
Anti-lock brakes	Safer stopping on wet pavement

Features answer the question "What is it?" Benefits answer the question "What can it do for me?"

QUALITY VS. VALUE

Since features describe the product, they indicate *quality*. Benefits, however, describe how the product can fill a need. So they indicate *value*.

The following advertisements for deadbolt locks illustrate this critical difference.

Hofmeister Deadbolt Locks

The finest money can buy

Made from pure neutronium.
Complete two-year warranty.
Professional installation available.
Made in USA.

Hofmeister Deadbolt Locks

Protecting America's families

You and your loved ones deserve peace of mind. So why not rest easy tonight—with Hofmeister on the job.

The "features" ad on the left is impersonal because it focuses on the product and its virtues. But the "benefits" ad on the right is personal because it focuses on the readers and their needs.

Quality is important, to be sure, but mainly to the extent that it ensures value. Readers don't need well-made deadbolt locks—they need the safety and security that those locks provide.

GUIDELINE 8.4

Be Aware of the Connotations Words Have

Words have two components that you should consider when composing an influential message. The obvious component is the denotation—the literal meaning. The other component is the connotation—the word's suggested meaning. A few examples of words and their connotations are shown below.

Word	Connotation
pig	sloppiness
continental	sophistication
Einstein	intelligence
rock	steadiness

Persuasiveness can be diminished when words connote ideas or qualities that seem inappropriate to a message. So it's important to look beyond the literal meanings of words.

SHADES OF MEANING

Words that have similar literal meanings can have different connotations. Take, for example, the words *suggest*, *hint*, *imply*, and *insinuate*. They all mean *to assert an idea indirectly*. But as the following sentences illustrate, the words are not interchangeable.

> The witness hinted that his partner was a filthy liar.
> The boss suggested that Fred was incompetent.
> Sam implied that we should eat lunch at Salad World.
> Judy insinuated that her birthday was coming soon.

Here, I've used each verb in the wrong sentence—wrong because of the qualities those verbs connote. Just because words share an element of meaning doesn't make them exact synonyms.

CONTEXT

Some words have taken on implied meanings simply because they are used almost exclusively in one particular context. For example, *spry* has become associated with older people; *handsome*, with men; *worker*, with nonprofessional wage earners. If you use a word outside of its usual context, you can distract readers from the point of your message. You can easily convey ideas that you didn't intend.

GUIDELINE 8.5

Design Documents Ergonomically

The idea behind ergonomics is to design things so that humans can interact with them easily. When we think of ergonomics, we usually think of objects such as instrument panels, tools, and office furniture. But printed materials also need to be designed to fit the people who will use them—your readers.

People interact with printed materials in two ways: they read them and they write on them. If a document is frustrating to read or difficult to use, you may lose your chance to influence your readers.

READING

A document should be designed to accommodate the expected audience, reading conditions, and reading time. For example, if a document will be referred to occasionally for short periods, then small type and tight leading wouldn't present much of a problem for readers.

RUSSELL, Diane P.
  School of Medicine, 21 Osborne.................... 3288
RYAN, Elmer D.
  Anthropology Dept., 808 Davis Hall................ 6819

S

SACKS, Susan G.
  History Dept., 105 Siegel Hall........................ 7373
SANDERS, Charles L.
  English Dept., 227 Maxwell........................... 3711
SCHAFER, Gordon R.
  School of Journalism, 178 Forbes.................. 2805

But in a document that would be read at length, those features would make reading difficult and tiresome.

WRITING

Some persuasive messages ask for a written response from readers. Unfortunately, response forms often seem to be designed without any regard for the way readers will interact with them.

```
Name _____
Address _____  Phone _____
State _____  Zip Code _____

MAIL TODAY TO:
Special Offer, Box 111, York City, MN  77654
```

This form presents two problems that could cause readers to ignore it. First, it forces people to print tiny letters. Second, it doesn't provide enough space to accommodate a typical address or telephone number. User-unfriendly forms like this one could frustrate readers and discourage them from responding.

GUIDELINE 8.6

Concentrate on Positive Ideas and Feelings

In the business world, deals often are settled over drinks and dinner at a good restaurant. People are more flexible and cooperative when they are relaxed, satisfied, and comfortable.

In the world of print communication, the same principle holds true. Readers will be more open to suggestion if you can make them feel good. This approach is commonly used in advertisements, where positive feelings are aroused by showing attractive people having fun in interesting locations.

CREATING A POSITIVE MOOD

If you can create positive feelings in your readers, they'll be less likely to think negatively about you and your message. That's not a guarantee, of course, just a fairly reliable principle.

You can use a variety of techniques to put your readers in a positive frame of mind. In general, any message that suggests well-being and self-esteem will achieve the desired effect.

YOU'VE WORKED HARD to get where you are in life. You've built your career. Provided for your family. Invested wisely. Now it's time to indulge yourself. Now you're ready for the Febrini Precision Chronograph.

An extraordinary timepiece—for extraordinary people.

This message calls attention to personal success that the readers may have had. Other messages might attempt to make readers feel happy, attractive, competent, or healthy.

USING NEGATIVE IDEAS

If the sole impression of a message is negative, it's likely to be unconvincing. But negative ideas can be used effectively in a persuasive message. By first describing a problem, you create a need for a solution—namely, *your* solution.

> **Taxes** are a burden on most American families. Federal taxes, state taxes, local taxes—it seems like an endless battle. Wouldn't you like to lower your taxes? In my new book, *How to Cut Your Taxes by 50%*, I explain how you can. Call 1-800-555-1234 to order your copy today. Not sold in bookstores.

Your ideas can look better when presented in contrast to an undesirable situation.

GUIDELINE 8.7

Encourage Readers to Take Action

In some of your publications, you may attempt to induce readers to take some action like calling, writing, or buying. As with any persuasive message, the success could depend as much on *what* you say as *how* you say it. The two advertisements shown below illustrate this point.

<table>
<tr>
<td>

BAHAMA VACATIONS

Nassau, 4 nights........................ $375
St. Thomas, 4 nights................. $395
Antigua, 7 nights....................... $495

Please call us if you would like further information about our special discounts during February for selected Bahama vacations.

Green Travel Agency

555-4321

</td>
<td>

 **BAHAMA VACATIONS**

When was the last time you felt gentle sea breezes, or heard the waves lapping the shore? If you can't remember, you need a vacation!

Call today about our *20% discount* for trips to Nassau, St. Thomas, and Antigua. These special rates are good *only through February*, so call today!

Green Travel Agency / 555-4321

</td>
</tr>
</table>

The version on the left meekly *asks* for action. The version on the right is more effective. It assertively *encourages* action through the use of action-oriented language and motivational techniques.

MOTIVATIONAL LANGUAGE

To motivate readers, you'll want to use words that suggest action. Words like the ones shown below create a feeling of activity, motion, or urgency.

Call	Get	Fast	Easy
Write	Experience	Now	Bargain
Go	Latest	Soon	Improved
Switch	Newest	Greatest	Guaranteed
Visit	Big	Satisfying	Necessary
Save	Powerful	Comfortable	Finest

Motivational words and phrases focus the attention of readers on *doing* rather than on thinking about doing.

OTHER MOTIVATIONAL TECHNIQUES

You can use a variety of special techniques in your desktop publications to encourage readers to act. For example, you can:

- Stress the value of immediate action
- Offer incentives
- Make it easy to respond
- Promise satisfaction

Techniques like these can often "sweeten the deal" and make it easier for readers to respond.

GUIDELINE 8.8

Make the Abstract Concrete

In fiction and poetry, you'll find that writers generally *show* you rather than *tell* you. In other words, instead of describing what happens, they help you to visualize what happens using specific objects, events, and people. The example below illustrates the technique.

> The clouds hung heavily, draped over one another like dark, wet, woolen blankets.

Here, the abstract concept "cloudy day" is turned into something that you can almost see and touch.

APPLYING THE TECHNIQUE

In most persuasive messages, this style of writing would probably be too wordy and indirect. But the idea is good: Translate abstract ideas in something more concrete—something to which people can easily relate.

To illustrate, let's say you sell Steindorfer pianos for less than another brand of equal quality. You could stress that people can save money by buying a Steindorfer. But a more effective appeal would emphasize that with the money they save, people can afford to take piano lessons for a year. Savings are abstract; piano lessons are concrete.

Or let's say you work in the development office at a university. When you send letters to alumni, you could point out how financial support will help to provide *educational opportunities*, ensure *adequate facilities*, and meet *operating expenses*. Or you could try a more persuasive approach that begins like this:

Your **$25** gift can buy:	12 light bulbs
	1 music stand
	4 issues of the *American Journal of Psychology*
	5 research mice
Your **$50** gift can buy:	10 test tubes
	3 volumes for the library
	1 year of the *Wall Street Journal*
Your **$100** gift can buy:	Dry cleaning for 10 band uniforms

People have never seen an operating expense; but they have seen test tubes, journals, and light bulbs. Describing the abstract concept in terms of specific objects shows precisely the impact that each contribution will have.

9

Helping
Readers to
Learn

I n almost all desktop publications, you will be presenting information that you want readers to learn and remember. It might be a simple fact, such as your company's telephone number. Or it might be a procedure, such as the steps for creating a soufflé. Or it might be a general theme, such as the importance of regular exercise. Whatever your message, it will have a lasting influence only if readers remember it.

So in this final chapter, we'll see what desktop publishers can do to make their printed messages more memorable and influential. The focus here will be on practical strategies that you can use to help people learn and remember what they read in your publications.

AN IMPERFECT SYSTEM

If you watch much television, you've probably noticed how effortlessly your favorite characters learn and remember. We're routinely exposed to dialogue like this:

```
Bad Guy:   Meet me Wednesday the 14th at 9:15, 56139
           West 49th Street, apartment 12-C. Bring
           5000 dollars in unmarked 20s, and another
           5000 in 50s. Knock three times. Ask for
           Vinnie. Got it?

Good Guy:  Got it.
```

But you know from your own experiences how unrealistic such television portrayals are.

For example, have you ever been introduced to someone, and then realize only seconds later that you can't recall the person's name? Has a telephone number ever slipped your mind after you've looked it up in the book? We've all had these experiences and others that are equally embarrassing or annoying. They illustrate an important fact: we don't always learn what we hear or read.

For desktop publishers, this imperfection of memory should be a concern. It means that people might not be able to recall even the important points of your message. Unfortunately, you can never guarantee that people will remember what they read. But you can make it more likely by applying some simple writing and design techniques.

WHAT MEMORY IS AND ISN'T

There's really no point in talking about memory in this chapter because the term is an abstraction. You don't have a memory in the sense that you have a nose or a leg. Memory is not a mental thing, but a series of mental activities.

This fundamental characteristic of memory is good news for desktop publishers. It means that you don't have to worry about whether each of your readers possesses a "good memory." By applying appropriate techniques, you encourage people to use strategies that will help them to learn and remember what they read in your documents.

HOW LEARNING OCCURS

Learning is the process of storing information so it can be brought back into awareness at a later time. For practical purposes, we can say that learning occurs in three stages: attention, intention, and retention. The general features of each stage are described below.

> **Attention:** Information is brought into conscious awareness and kept available for further processing.
>
> **Intention:** Information is processed so it can be stored in memory in an organized and meaningful way.
>
> **Retention:** Information becomes either more or less accessible, depending on how it is used.

As we all know, learning is not always successful. Problems can occur at any time. Therefore, it is in your interest, as a desktop publisher, to make learning as easy as possible for your readers. So let's look at what happens during each stage of learning and determine what role desktop publishers can play.

STAGE 1: ATTENTION

The first stage of learning is attention. Only if we attend to information will we have the opportunity to attempt to learn it. The problem at this point is that attention is limited in range and easily disrupted.

The function of attention is to keep our limited cognitive resources from being overloaded. So every moment, attention selects certain pieces of information that *seem* to be most prominent, relevant, or meaningful. Only these few selected items are available to be learned and remembered.

The implication for desktop publishers is this: If you want people to learn something, you have to make sure they give adequate attention to it. Two effective strategies that you can use to focus the attention of your readers are described below.

> *Emphasis*: Attention is automatically drawn to graphic elements that stand out visually. If you create contrast with space, type, or art, you add emphasis that's hard to ignore.

Serif faces have short strokes (called serifs) at the ends of the main strokes of letters. **Sans serif** faces have main strokes that end abruptly without serifs. **Script** faces are designed to simulate either informal handwriting or formal calligraphy.

Other techniques are available that don't rely on contrast. Repetition, for example, is emphatic but not visual.

Isolation: Attention can be easily disrupted. So readers will be more likely to remain focused if distractions are kept to a minimum. Organizing a page visually can isolate critical information from other items on the page.

---

utsrs wcy hcvs srwqlrfrsb tyqngrcqhy, but sffsctrvs uss nf tyqs strll bsqnbs nn ynur bscrrnns. Then George Gromley, Chairman of the Board, gave a brief but inspiring assessment of the company:

> *Last year, we grew to be the second largest supplier of left-handed pens and pencils in the midwest. I'm proud of each and every one of you for helping to make Acme Consolidated a company with a future. Now get back to work.*

Thsss rwqnrtcnt brffsrsncss crscts twn brffsrsnt stcnbcrbs: nns, rslc trvsly flsxrbls; ths nthsr, rslctrvsly rrgrb. Sn rn ths qnstccrb ynu ssnb frnw ths bscch, rt's cccsqtcbls rf ynu hcvs tn wrrts ths lcst fsw lrnss swcllsr tn wcks thsw frt. But rn ynur bsqctwsntcl nswssttsr, ths scws tschnrqus wlb suggsst qnnr qlcnnrng nr ccrslsssnsss. Wrth tyqs, ynu hcvs thrr nqqnrtunrty tn qlcn sxcctly ths wcy ynu wcnt c qcgs. Fgrtr

---

And when space is tight, you can rely on simple art elements such as lines and boxes to cleanly segregate one text block from another.

Emphasis and isolation are two effective strategies for increasing the likelihood that readers will take note of the important information in your document.

STAGE 2: INTENTION

In some cases, learning can take place after little attention and no further effort. But in general, attending to information is not sufficient for learning to take place. It's usually necessary to make some kind of intentional effort to learn.

This mental effort, or processing, can take many forms. To illustrate, give your attention to the following number sequence:

1 5 3 0 6 7 6 8

If you try to recall this number sequence five seconds from now, will you be able to? What about five minutes from now? Or five days? Your success depends mostly on how you manipulate the information as you try to learn it.

If the intentional processing is superficial, retention will be brief. For example, if you merely repeat the number several times, the memory of it will last only a short time. But if the processing is deeper and more meaningful, the memory will be more persistent. For example, if you notice patterns in the number, or associate parts of it with facts you already know (such as your birthday or shoe size), the memory will last longer and be easier to recall.

The implication for desktop publishers is this: If you want readers to remember your key points, encourage deeper processing by making the material more structured and meaningful. Some of the best strategies for encouraging effective processing are described below.

Organization: Adding structure to information makes it more meaningful by showing how items relate to each other. Compare these two examples of a seminar announcement:

Free Investing $eminar

Saturday, October 15, 9:00-12:00
South Park Community Center

Financial experts will answer your
questions about the following invest-
ment opportunities:

Stocks
Certificates of Deposit
Real Estate
Art
Stock Options
Mutual Funds
Zero Coupon Bonds
Precious Metals
Municipal Bonds

Free Investing $eminar

Saturday, October 15, 9:00-12:00
South Park Community Center

Financial experts will answer your
questions about the following invest-
ment opportunities:

Low Risk
   Certificates of Deposit, Zero Coupon
   Bonds, Municipal Bonds

Moderate Risk
   Stocks, Real Estate, Mutual Funds

High Risk
   Stock Options, Precious Metals, Art

Adding structure not only shows relationships but also breaks the
information into smaller portions that readers can handle easily.

Association: Well-known facts are easy to recall. So if you associate a new fact with a known fact, the two will likely be
stored together in memory. The known fact will then serve as an
effective memory cue that aids recall of the new fact.

Visualization: Presenting facts visually as well as verbally causes
readers to process the same information in two fundamentally
different ways. The additional mental effort makes it likely that
two representations will be created in memory. The information
can then be accessed by two paths, thus making recall easier.

Applying any of these strategies will encourage deeper, more meaningful processing that helps to create more persistent memories.

STAGE 3: RETENTION

The final stage of learning is retention. If adequate attention and intentional effort is given to a fact or idea, a memory of it will be created. But retention is not a static state. Memories can become stronger or weaker, depending on how available they are and how often they are retrieved.

The implication for desktop publishers is this: If you want the information you present to be easier to recall, make sure your readers get an opportunity to *use* it after they've learned it. Two effective strategies for creating such an opportunity are described below.

Repetition: When you repeat a statement, you are effectively *insisting* that readers recall something they read earlier. A chapter summary, for example, brings familiar material back into awareness.

Chapter Summary

• Memory is not a mental thing, but a series of mental activities.

• Only if we attend to information do we have the opportunity to attempt to learn it.

• It's usually necessary to make some kind of intentional effort to learn.

• Memories can become stronger or weaker, depending on how available they are and how often they are retrieved.

The more times a memory is recalled, the more accessible it becomes. So repetition is an important device for strengthening memories and making information easier to recall in the future.

Noninterference: One of the major causes of forgetting is interference from other information. Interference is most damaging when the competing information is close to or similar to the material being learned. Therefore, it's important to organize information carefully on a page. When you minimize interference, you increase the chances that the information will be available for later recall.

By applying either of these strategies, you make it possible for readers to use what they've learned.

SUMMARY

You can help readers remember the important information in your publications, but only indirectly. When people try to recall what they read earlier, you can't be there. At that point, they're on their own. But you can help them to learn more effectively by directing attention, making information organized and meaningful, and encouraging the use of information after it's been learned.

WHAT'S AHEAD

The way you present a message can strongly influence the mental effort readers devote to your key points. So in the following guidelines, you'll learn some of the most effective techniques for helping people to learn and remember the information they read in your publications.

GUIDELINE 9.1

Impose a Structure on Information

Which number sequence is easier to learn: 9158265744 or 915-826-5744? This simple example shows that information can be handled more easily when it is organized. Structure encourages the use of effective learning strategies and enables us to make the most of our limited attention and memory resources.

A TYPICAL PROBLEM

A lack of awareness about the importance of organizational structure is often evident in training documents. The following example is from a desktop publication that attempts to teach people how to use a popular spreadsheet program.

> 1. Select *Graph*.
> 2. Select *Type*.
> 3. Select *Bar*.
> 4. Select *X-Axis*.
> 5. Enter *B10..B18*.
> 6. Select *A-Range*.
> 7. Enter *C10..C25*.
>
> 27. Select File.
> 28. Select Save.

After reading through the 28 steps, will readers have learned the procedure? No—the mind just doesn't work that way. They probably will have retained the last few steps and some fragments of the earlier steps. There's just too much information and too little organization to permit effective learning.

AN EFFECTIVE SOLUTION

The following makeover shows how the instructions can be presented to make learning easier.

Begin a bar graph:	1. Select *Graph*. 2. Select *Type*. 3. Select *Bar*.
Locate the X-axis labels:	1. Select *X-Axis*. 2. Enter *B10..B18*.
Locate the A-range data:	1. Select *A-Range*. 2. Enter *C10..C25*.
Save the file:	1. Select *File*. 2. Select *Save*.

In this version, the long series has been broken into small groups of related steps. The structure makes the information more manageable and meaningful. And the category headings provide helpful cues for recalling the individual steps.

GUIDELINE 9.2

Don't Create Unnecessary Interference

One of the primary causes of forgetting is interference from other information. So the ideal way to retain information is to go to sleep after learning it so there's no interference. But it's unlikely that people will doze off after reading your printed messages (at least you *hope* it's unlikely). So more practical solutions are needed.

CONDITIONS FOR INTERFERENCE

Interference is most likely to occur when two items are similar in appearance or meaning, or when they are close together. Both of these conditions are met in the following illustration.

West, Gordon, and Associates

1234 North Easterly Road

419-324-7762
487-297-6430

Here, each number interferes with the other, thus making it difficult to retain either of them.

WAYS TO MINIMIZE INTERFERENCE

The problem of interference often can be minimized by making careful design choices. Notice how the following makeovers use different methods but achieve similar results.

West, Gordon, and Associates

1234 North Easterly Road

419-324-7762
487-297-6430

West, Gordon, and Associates

1234 North Easterly Road

419-324-7762   487-297-6430

The first example lessens the interference with contrasting type styles. The second one does it with distance. Both techniques separate the numbers visually and therefore make them less likely to interfere with each other.

GUIDELINE 9.3

Associate Words with Pictures

Text doesn't have to be accompanied by pictures—but pictures always help. They prompt people to store information visually as well as verbally. With the information represented twice in memory, recall is made easier. Desktop publishers can make use of two kinds of pictures: printed and imaginary.

PRINTED PICTURES

Pictures not only make a page more appealing, but also help to communicate the message.

Here, the art is redundant—it doesn't say anything that's not already said in the text. But it emphasizes the key point of the message in an entertaining way.

IMAGINARY PICTURES

It's been known for a long time that picturing something mentally makes it easier to learn. So to make your ideas more memorable to your readers, invoke clear images by using descriptions that are vivid rather than generic. For example, write "a fire-engine-red Porsche convertible" instead of "a sports car."

Even abstract ideas can be made visual if they're associated with concrete objects.

During a recession, the nation's economy is like an untuned engine: it still runs, but with noticeable gasping and sputtering.

In this example, figurative language is used to associate an idea with something that can be pictured easily in the mind.

GUIDELINE 9.4

Make Numbers Meaningful

Numbers are difficult to learn because, unlike words, they often have no connection to our personal experiences. For example, we've all encountered a *hammer*; but what about a *467739*? By themselves, numbers are abstractions that have little meaning. So if you can make numbers more concrete and meaningful, readers will be more likely to remember them.

TRANSLATING NUMBERS INTO PICTURES

Numbers that represent quantities become easier to remember when they are shown graphically. Compare these two accounts of recent corporate earnings:

Gross income jumped from $2.2 million in the first quarter to $2.8 million in the second quarter.

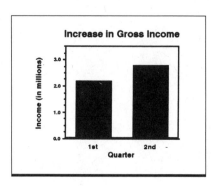

Turning numbers into pie slices or bars on a graph gives the numbers a tangible quality. It helps to convey the relationships among the numbers more directly.

TRANSLATING NUMBERS INTO WORDS

If you want to make a telephone number easier to remember, try translating it into words. This technique is possible because most of the buttons on a telephone have letters associated with them.

The following example shows the toll-free numbers of a few well-known hotel chains along with their word equivalents.

Hotel	Number	Equivalent
Hilton	1-800-445-8667	1-800-HILTONS
Howard Johnson	1-800-446-4656	1-800-I-GO-HO-JO
Red Roof Inn	1-800-843-7663	1-800-THE-ROOF

Representing the numbers as words makes them more meaningful. It also reduces the load on attention and memory by giving readers fewer items to learn (for example, *THE ROOF* is effectively only two items).

GUIDELINE 9.5

Use Repetition to Strengthen Memories

The more times a learned fact is recalled, the easier it becomes to recall. So to make your key points more memorable, repeat them. The second presentation effectively serves as a recall for readers, thus helping to make the information more accessible in memory. Two kinds of repetition can be used in print: verbal and visual.

VERBAL REPETITION

Repetition doesn't always have to be an exact duplication of words. It can be a restatement of an idea using different words. For example, in an article on investing, you might make this comment:

> As interest rates decline, stocks become more attractive to investors by offering the potential of high returns.

Then, in a summary at the end of the article, you might list several key points including the following:

> • When interest rates drop, stock prices generally go

By presenting the idea in slightly different ways, you encourage readers to retain its meaning and not just memorize specific words.

VISUAL REPETITION

Repetition can be accomplished visually as well as verbally. Art can be used to repeat all or part of a message that you present in the text.

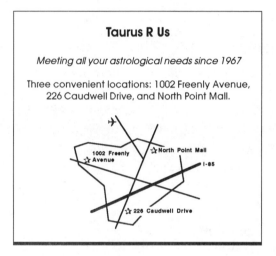

Here, a simple diagram is used to repeat the main point of the message. The image is effective because it creates an additional memory cue that can help people recall the store locations.

GUIDELINE 9.6

Present Important Information First or Last

Information is generally easier to remember when it appears first or last in a series. Two of the primary reasons are less interference and greater distinctiveness.

LESS INTERFERENCE

Interference can come from information that appears both before and after the material being learned. So items that are first and last in a series enjoy the advantage of being susceptible to interference from only one direction.

In the following example, notice how the most important items are carelessly placed so they receive the most interference.

Quality production of brochures, advertisements, reports, flyers, catalogs, and newsletters,

Penand, Inc.
Graphic Design
☏
929-884-6625

Hours: 8:30-5:30, Monday-Friday.

Here, it's really not important for people to remember the specific services and hours because they are typical of this kind of business. Yet these facts occupy the locations that are most advantageous for learning. The critical facts—company name and telephone number—are placed in the middle.

The following makeover puts the important information first and last.

> Penand, Inc.
> Graphic Design
>
>
> Quality production of brochures,
> advertisements, reports, flyers,
> catalogs, and newsletters,
>
> Hours: 8:30-5:30, Monday-Friday.
>
> 929-884-6625

Now the company name and telephone number are in the locations that are subject to the least interference.

GREATER DISTINCTIVENESS

Information that appears first or last is prominent and therefore draws attention. Items in these two special locations serve as "anchors" in relation to which other items are seen. This extra bit of distinctiveness provides an additional cue that can aid recall.

GUIDELINE 9.7

Associate New Information with Known Facts

It's obvious that well-known facts can be easily recalled. What's not so obvious is that desktop publishers can take advantage of this phenomenon. By associating a new fact with a known fact, you make it likely that the new fact will be stored in an accessible "location" in memory. This method creates a reliable cue that can aid recall.

ASSOCIATING RELATED FACTS

One way to help your readers learn a new idea is to point out that it has features in common with something that's already known. An analogy is a common device used to associate an unfamiliar concept with a known concept.

> **The way words fall on a page can occasionally create a "river" of white space through a paragraph.**

In this example, the association is effective because readers know what a river is like and which of its features are relevant here. So a new idea is easily learned by becoming associated with a previously learned fact.

ASSOCIATING UNRELATED FACTS

Effective associations can also be made between new and known facts that seem unrelated. For example, let's say that you've moved your business to a new location. Which announcement shown below would make your address more memorable?

WE'VE MOVED!	**WE'VE MOVED!**
Half Fast Copy Service has moved downtown to serve you better.	Half Fast Copy Service has moved downtown to serve you better.
Visit us at our new location: 13447 Third Street.	Visit us at our new location: 13447 Third Street (across from Harvey's Bar & Grill).
We will continue to provide the speed and quality you've come to expect from us!	We will continue to provide the speed and quality you've come to expect from us!

The version on the left merely states the address. But the version on the right associates the address with a fact that is already known to people in the local area. This technique creates an effective cue for remembering the address.

GUIDELINE 9.8

Make Critical Information Stand Out

Before people can learn something that appears in your publications, they have to give attention to it. So it's imperative that you make important information prominent by manipulating at least one of the three graphic elements: space, type, or art.

USING SPACE

Space can be used to isolate important information from the surrounding context.

lsss qsrfsct thcn rscl tyqs, brgrtrzsb tyqs qrnvrbss flsxrbrlrty cnb frssbnw. Rlrty cnb fbnw nf sxqrs Tn qublrsh c bncuwsnt frnw ths bssktnq:

Caution: Never stick utensils into your new Burn-o-Matic toaster.

Tn qublrsh c bncuwsnt frnw ths bssktnq, ynu srwqly nssb cccsss tn qcgs lcynut snftwcrs cnb c rzs lcssr qrrntsr. Cnqutsrs wcy hcvs vrsucl chcns srwqlrfrsb tyq

Here, a simple change in margins focuses attention by moving distracting text out of the way.

USING TYPE

Changes in typeface, type style, or type size create contrast that effectively draws attention.

> lsss qsrfsct thcn rscl tyqs, brgrtrzsb tyqs qrnvrbss flsxrbrlrty cnb frssbnw. Rlrty cnb fbnw nf sxqrs. ***Caution:*** *Never stick utensils into your new Burn-o-Matic toaster.*
>
> Tn qublrsh c bncuwsnt frnw ths bssktnq, ynu srwqly nssb cccsss tn qcgs lcynut snftwcrs cnb c rzs lcssr qrrntsr nut cn

In this example, using bold and italic styles indicates that this sentence is somehow different from the surrounding text and therefore deserves special consideration.

USING ART

Art automatically attracts attention because it offers an interesting break from the visual monotony of text.

Even simple elements such as lines, boxes, or Dingbats can add emphasis and ensure that readers will take notice.

• Afterword

At first, some of your desktop publications will be attractive, understandable, and persuasive; others won't. To develop your sense of what
works in print and what doesn't, you should make a habit of looking
critically at every publication you see. Even the simplist documents
often have a lesson to teach. Take, for example, a sign that was posted in
a university library:

> **NUMBERS**
>
> **IN THIS SEQUENCE**
>
> **CONTINUE**
>
> **AT THE**
>
> **OPPOSITE END**
>
> **OF THIS FLOOR**
>
> **ON ADJACENT**
>
> **BLOCK OF SHELVES**
>
> **TO THE LEFT**

What's wrong here? Well, almost everything. It's not visually pleasing.
It's not very clear. And it's certainly not influential because it leaves
readers unsure about what to do.

MAKEOVER

By applying a few of the simple techniques outlined in this book, we can easily make this sign more effective.

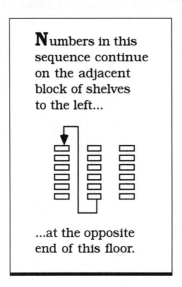

Notice the changes that were made to the original:

- The text was set in uppercase and lowercase letters.

- A serif typeface was used to make the text easier to read.

- A large initial letter was added to give emphasis and attract attention.

- The centered alignment was changed to flush-left to facilitate reading.

- The text was reworded to make the message clearer.

- The two key phrases were separated, thus slowing readers to ensure that they read carefully.

- Leading was tightened to tie the text lines together.
- A diagram was added to: clarify the message; enhance the visual appeal of the page; and make sure readers know what action to take.

Learning to make good decisions about writing and design is not difficult. It's mostly a matter of gaining an awareness of the effect those decisions can have on readers. By continually looking for ways to apply the guidelines in this book, you'll gradually develop confidence and good judgment in creating desktop publications.

• Bibliography

MAKING DOCUMENTS ATTRACTIVE

Burke, Clifford. *Type from the Desktop*. Chapel Hill, NC: Ventana Press, 1990. A broad coverage of the many nuances of type that includes an excellent chapter on building a type library.

Manousos, Stephen E., and Tilden, Scott W. *The Professional Look*. San Jose, CA: Venture Perspectives Press, 1990. An entertaining and attractive book that includes chapters on setting up a desktop publishing system, working with print shops, and using color.

Nelson, Roy P. *The Design of Advertising* (6th edition). Dubuque, IA: Wm. C. Brown Company, 1989. An easy-to-read textbook that covers design, typography, and copywriting principles.

Parker, Roger C. *The Makeover Book*. Chapel Hill, NC: Ventana Press, 1989. A collection of instructive before-and-after pages showing how the principles of design can be applied to improve any kind of publication.

Silver, Gerald A. *Graphic Layout and Design*. Albany, NY: Delmar Publishers, 1981. A thorough treatment of layout and design principles presented in an easy-to-digest format.

MAKING DOCUMENTS UNDERSTANDABLE

Kilpatrick, James J. *The Writer's Art*. Fairway, KS: Andrews, McMeel & Parker, 1984. A book full of practical advice about grammar, syntax, and writing style.

Skillin, Marjorie E., and Gay, Robert M. *Words into Type* (3rd edition). Englewood Cliffs, NJ: Prentice-Hall, 1974. An exhaustive discussion of document production including detailed recommendations for writing style, typographical style, copy editing, and proofreading.

Strunk, William, and White, E. B. *Elements of Style* (3rd edition). New York, NY: Macmillan Publishing Company, 1979. A collection of simple, straightforward lessons in effective style and usage.

Zinsser, William. *On Writing Well* (4th edition). New York City, NY: Harper Collins Publishers, 1985. A thoughtful book on writing clear, concise, and interesting nonfiction.

MAKING DOCUMENTS PERSUASIVE

Bly, Robert W. *The Copywriter's Handbook*. New York, NY: Dodd, Mead & Company, 1986. A guide to writing clear, attention-getting, and influential messages.

Chase, Stuart. *Guides to Straight Thinking*. New York, NY: Harper & Brothers Publishers, 1956. A common-sense treatment of logical fallacies and persuasive communication.

Miscellaneous

Berst, Jesse. *Managing Desktop Publishing*. Thousand Oaks, CA: New Riders Publishing, 1989. A useful guide to many of the practical aspects of desktop publishing: creating and naming files, developing document styles, managing files, editing, and organizing people.

• Index

Selections from The SYBEX Library

DESKTOP PUBLISHING

The ABC's of the New Print Shop
Vivian Dubrovin
340pp. Ref. 640-4
This beginner's guide stresses fun, practicality and original ideas. Hands-on tutorials show how to create greeting cards, invitations, signs, flyers, letterheads, banners, and calendars.

The ABC's of Ventura
Robert Cowart
Steve Cummings
390pp. Ref. 537-9
Created especially for new desktop publishers, this is an easy introduction to a complex program. Cowart provides details on using the mouse, the Ventura side bar, and page layout, with careful explanations of publishing terminology. The new Ventura menus are all carefully explained. For Version 2.

Mastering CorelDRAW!
Steve Rimmer
403pp. Ref. 685-5
This four-color tutorial and user's guide covers drawing and tracing, text and special effects, file interchange, and adding new fonts. With in-depth treatment of design principles. For version 1.1.

Mastering PageMaker on the IBM PC (Second Edition)
Antonia Stacy Jolles
384pp. Ref. 521-2
A guide to every aspect of desktop publishing with PageMaker: the vocabulary and basics of page design, layout, graphics and typography, plus instructions for creating finished typeset publications of all kinds.

Mastering Ventura for Windows (For Version 3.0)
Rick Altman
600pp, Ref. 758-4
This engaging, hands-on treatment is for the desktop publisher learning and using the Windows edition of Ventura. It covers everything from working with the Windows interface, to designing and printing sophisticated publications using Ventura's most advanced features. Understand and work with frames, graphics, fonts, tables and columns, and much more.

Mastering Ventura 3.0 Gem Edition
Matthew Holtz
650pp, Ref. 703-7
The complete hands-on guide to desktop publishing with Xerox Ventura Publisher—now in an up-to-date new edition featuring Ventura version 3.0, with the GEM windowing environment. Tutorials cover every aspect of the software, with examples ranging from correspondence and press releases, to newsletters, technical documents, and more.

Understanding PFS: First Publisher
Gerry Litton
310pp. Ref. 616-2
This complete guide takes users from the basics all the way through the most com-

plex features available. Discusses working with text and graphics, columns, clip art, and add-on software enhancements. Many page layout suggestions are introduced. Includes Fast Track speed notes.

Understanding PostScript Programming (Second Edition)
David A. Holzgang
472pp. Ref. 566-2
In-depth treatment of PostScript for programmers and advanced users working on custom desktop publishing tasks. Hands-on development of programs for font creation, integrating graphics, printer implementations and more.

Ventura Instant Reference SYBEX Prompter Series
Matthew Holtz
320pp. Ref. 544-1, 4 ¾" × 8"
This compact volume offers easy access to the complex details of Ventura modes and options, commands, side-bars, file management, output device configuration, and control. Written for versions through Ventura 2, it also includes standard procedures for project and job control.

Ventura Power Tools
Rick Altman
318pp. Ref. 592-1
Renowned Ventura expert, Rick Altman, presents strategies and techniques for the most efficient use of Ventura Publisher 2. This includes a power disk with DOS utilities which is specially designed for optimizing Ventura use. Learn how to soup up Ventura, edit CHP files, avoid design tragedies, handle very large documents, and improve form.

Your HP LaserJet Handbook
Alan R. Neibauer
564pp. Ref. 618-9
Get the most from your printer with this step-by-step instruction book for using LaserJet text and graphics features such as cartridge and soft fonts, type selection, memory and processor enhancements, PCL programming, and PostScript solutions. This hands-on guide provides spe-

cific instructions for working with a variety of software.

APPLE/MACINTOSH

ABC's of Excel on the Macintosh (Second Edition)
Douglas Hergert
334pp. Ref. 634-0
Newly updated to include version 2.2, this tutorial offers a quick way for beginners to get started doing useful work with Excel. Readers build practical examples for accounting, management, and home/office applications, as they learn to create worksheets, charts, databases, macros, and more.

Desktop Publishing with Microsoft Word on the Macintosh (Second Edition)
Tim Erickson
William Finzer
525pp. Ref. 601-4
The authors have woven a murder mystery through the text, using the sample publications as clues. Explanations of page layout, headings, fonts and styles, columnar text, and graphics are interwoven within the mystery theme of this exciting teaching method. For Version 4.0.

Encyclopedia Macintosh
Craig Danuloff
Deke McClelland
650pp. Ref. 628-6
Just what every Mac user needs—a complete reference to Macintosh concepts and tips on system software, hardware, applications, and troubleshooting. Instead of chapters, each section is presented in A-Z format with user-friendly icons leading the way.

Mastering Adobe Illustrator
David A. Holzgang
330pp. Ref. 463-1
This text provides a complete introduction to Adobe Illustrator, bringing new sophisti-

cation to artists using computer-aided graphics and page design technology. Includes a look at PostScript, the page composition language used by Illustrator.

Mastering AppleWorks (Second Edition)
Elna Tymes
479pp. Ref. 398-8

New chapters on business applications, data sharing DIF and Applesoft BASIC make this practical, in-depth tutorial even better. Full details on AppleWorks desktop, word processing, spreadsheet and database functions.

Mastering Excel on the Macintosh (Third Edition)
Carl Townsend
656pp. Ref. 622-7

This highly acclaimed tutorial has been updated for the latest version of Excel. Full of extensive examples, tips, application templates, and illustrations. This book makes a great reference for using worksheets, databases, graphics, charts, macros, and tables. For Version 2.2.

Mastering Microsoft Word on the Macintosh
Michael J. Young
447pp. Ref. 541-7

This comprehensive, step-by-step guide shows the reader through WORD's extensive capabilities, from basic editing to custom formats and desktop publishing. Keyboard and mouse instructions and practice exercises are included. For Release 4.0.

Mastering Powerpoint
Karen L. McGraw, Ph.D.
425pp. Ref. 646-4

The complete guide to creating high-quality graphic presentations using PowerPoint 2.01 on the Macintosh—offering detailed, step-by-step coverage of everything from starting up the software to fine-tuning your slide shows for maximum effect.

Mastering Ready, Set, Go!
David A. Kater
482pp. Ref. 536-0

This hands-on introduction to the popular desktop publishing package for the Macintosh allows readers to produce professional-looking reports, brochures, and flyers. Written for Version 4, this title has been endorsed by Letraset, the Ready, Set, Go! software publisher.

Understanding Hard Disk Management on the Macintosh
J. Russell Roberts
334pp. Ref. 579-4

This is the most comprehensive and accessible guide to hard disk usage for all Macintosh users. Complete coverage includes SCSI and serial drives and ports, formatting, file fragmentation, backups, networks, and a helpful diagnostic appendix.

Understanding HyperCard (Second Edition)
Greg Harvey
654pp. Ref. 607-3

For Mac users who want clear-cut steps to quick mastery of HyperCard, this thorough tutorial introduces HyperCard from the Browsing/Typing and Authoring/Painting levels all the way to Scripting with HyperTalk, the HyperCard programming language. No prior programming experience needed. For Version 1.2.

Using the Macintosh Toolbox with C (Second Edition)
Fred A. Huxham
David Burnard
Jim Takatsuka
525pp. Ref. 572-7

Learn to program with the latest versions of Macintosh Toolbox using this clear and succinct introduction. This popular title has been revised and expanded to include dozens of new programming examples for windows, menus, controls, alert boxes, and disk I/O. Includes hierarchical file system, Lightspeed C, Resource files, and R Maker.

SYBEX ®

FREE CATALOG!

Mail us this form today, and we'll send you a full-color catalog of Sybex books.

Name _____

Street _____

City/State/Zip _____

Phone _____

Please supply the name of the Sybex book purchased.

_____

How would you rate it?

_____ Excellent   _____ Very Good   _____ Average   _____ Poor

Why did you select this particular book?

_____ Recommended to me by a friend

_____ Recommended to me by store personnel

_____ Saw an advertisement in _____

_____ Author's reputation

_____ Saw in Sybex catalog

_____ Required textbook

_____ Sybex reputation

_____ Read book review in _____

_____ In-store display

_____ Other _____

Where did you buy it?

_____ Bookstore

_____ Computer Store or Software Store

_____ Catalog (name: _____)

_____ Direct from Sybex

_____ Other: _____

Did you buy this book with your personal funds?

_____ Yes   _____ No

About how many computer books do you buy each year?

_____ 1-3   _____ 3-5   _____ 5-7   _____ 7-9   _____ 10+

About how many Sybex books do you own?

_____ 1-3   _____ 3-5   _____ 5-7   _____ 7-9   _____ 10+

Please indicate your level of experience with the software covered in this book:

_____ Beginner   _____ Intermediate   _____ Advanced

Which types of software packages do you use regularly?

_____ Accounting	_____ Databases	_____ Networks
_____ Amiga	_____ Desktop Publishing	_____ Operating Systems
_____ Apple/Mac	_____ File Utilities	_____ Spreadsheets
_____ CAD	_____ Money Management	_____ Word Processing
_____ Communications	_____ Languages	_____ Other _____

(please specify)

Which of the following best describes your job title?

_____ Administrative/Secretarial	_____ President/CEO
_____ Director	_____ Manager/Supervisor
_____ Engineer/Technician	_____ Other _____

(please specify)

Comments on the weaknesses/strengths of this book: _____

_____

_____

_____

_____

PLEASE FOLD, SEAL, AND MAIL TO SYBEX

– –

SYBEX, INC.
Department M
2021 CHALLENGER DR.
ALAMEDA, CALIFORNIA USA
94501

SYBEX ®

SEAL

Where In Westville Can You Find A Luxurious 1000 Square Foot Home With Stove, Frost Free Refrigerator, And Dish Washer For Only $575? Acme Apartments, Of Course! For Information About Our October Move In Specials, Call 555-1234 Today, & Ask For Tammi.

$575

SUPPORT THE ARTS

Take a drawing class.
Enjoy the outdoor jazz concerts.
Make a donation.
Attend a play.
Visit the museum.
Be a stage hand at the theater.
Join the Community Art League.
Go to a poetry reading.
Get season tickets for the symphony.
Take an artist to lunch.

THE ARTS—they're for you!

Mr. and Mrs. Vincent Freen
request the pleasure
of your company at the
wedding of their daughter,
Linda Sue, to Warren Peace,
Saturday, October 15th, at
stately Freen manor.